POPE BENEDICT XVI

Recent Titles in Greenwood Biographies

Pancho Villa: A Biography
Alejandro Quintana

Michelle Obama: A Biography
Alma Halbert Bond

Lady Gaga: A Biography
Paula Johanson

Bono: A Biography
David Kootnikoff

Henry Louis Gates, Jr.: A Biography
Meg Greene

Robert E. Lee: A Biography
Brian C. Melton

Ulysses S. Grant: A Biography
Robert B. Broadwater

Thurgood Marshall: A Biography
Glenn L. Starks and F. Erik Brooks

Katy Perry: A Biography
Kimberly Dillon Summers

Sonia Sotomayor: A Biography
Meg Greene

Stephen Colbert: A Biography
Catherine M. Andronik

William T. Sherman: A Biography
Robert P. Broadwater

POPE BENEDICT XVI

A Biography

Joann F. Price

GREENWOOD BIOGRAPHIES

GREENWOOD

AN IMPRINT OF ABC-CLIO, LLC
Santa Barbara, California • Denver, Colorado • Oxford, England

Library of Congress Cataloging-in-Publication Data

Price, Joann F.
  Pope Benedict XVI : a biography / Joann F. Price.
    pages cm. — (Greenwood biographies)
  Includes bibliographical references and index.
  ISBN 978-0-313-35123-5 (alk. paper) — ISBN 978-0-313-35124-2 (ebook)
1. Benedict XVI, Pope, 1927– I. Title.
  BX1378.6.P75 2013
  282.092—dc23
  [B]   2013000310

ISBN: 978-0-313-35123-5
EISBN: 978-0-313-35124-2

17 16 15 14 13   1 2 3 4 5

This book is also available on the World Wide Web as an eBook.
Visit www.abc-clio.com for details.

Greenwood
An Imprint of ABC-CLIO, LLC

ABC-CLIO, LLC
130 Cremona Drive, P.O. Box 1911
Santa Barbara, California 93116-1911

This book is printed on acid-free paper ∞

Manufactured in the United States of America

To Bob, my blessing, whose love and humor continue to astound me.
To Carol, whose sheer valor and keen intellect enlighten my days.

CONTENTS

Series Foreword   ix

Preface   xi

Introduction   xiii

Timeline: Events in the Life of Pope Benedict XVI   xix

Chapter 1   An Introduction to the Vatican and to the Popes
            of the Modern Era   1

Chapter 2   The Early Years   25

Chapter 3   Entering the Priesthood   45

Chapter 4   Pastoral Ministry, Doctorate Degree, and
            a Theologian   53

Chapter 5   The Path to Rome   63

Chapter 6   The Prefect of the Congregation for the Doctrine
            of the Faith   81

Chapter 7   The Ascendance of Pope Benedict XVI   91

CONTENTS

Chapter 8   The Perspectives of Pope Benedict XVI   113

Conclusion   129

Addendum   135

Bibliography   143

Index   147

SERIES FOREWORD

In response to school and library needs, ABC-CLIO publishes this distinguished series of full-length biographies specifically for student use. Prepared by field experts and professionals, these engaging biographies are tailored for students who need challenging, yet accessible biographies. Ideal for school assignments and student research, the length, format, and subject areas are designed to meet educators' requirements and students' interests.

ABC-CLIO offers an extensive selection of biographies spanning all curriculum-related subject areas, including social studies, the sciences, literature and the arts, history and politics, and popular culture, covering public figures and famous personalities from all time periods and backgrounds, both historic and contemporary, who have made an impact on American and/or world culture. The subjects of these biographies were chosen based on comprehensive feedback from librarians and educators. Consideration was given to both curriculum relevance and inherent interest. Readers will find a wide array of subject choices, from fascinating entertainers, such as Miley Cyrus and Lady Gaga, to inspiring leaders, such as John F. Kennedy and Nelson Mandela, from the greatest athletes of our time, such as Michael Jordan and Muhammad Ali, to the most amazing success stories of our day, such as J.K. Rowling and Oprah Winfrey.

While the emphasis is on fact, not glorification, the books are meant to be fun to read. Each volume provides in-depth information about the subject's life, from birth through childhood, the teen years, and adulthood. A thorough account relates family background and education, traces personal and professional influences, and explores the individual's struggles, accomplishments, and contributions. A timeline highlights the most significant life events against an historical perspective. Bibliographies supplement the reference value of each volume.

PREFACE

The purpose of this biography is to enlighten the reader about the life of Pope Benedict XVI, to hear this pope's words, to understand his directives, and to appreciate what he profoundly believes. This biography will enlighten why it is important to understand how and why Benedict XVI is known as the great giver and the absolute leader of the Catholic Church and how he gave his very life, from the time he was a young boy, to serve the Church through his faith and beliefs. The pope that readers will meet here is a parish priest, a professor, a disciple, and a man who believes that his faith in his God is the key to his own happiness and to the happiness of all. The reader will learn of Benedict XVI's determination to reform the papacy by returning it to its evangelical ideals, tracing what the Church stands for, all the way back to the first pope; and how world and religious history and accepting the position of pope at the age of 78 have influenced his papacy and dictated the direction of the Church.

To read a biography of any pope and certainly in reading the story of this pope, it is important to understand the role of the Vatican, the Holy See, and the popes who came before Benedict XVI, especially those of the 20th century, known as the modern popes of the modern era of the Catholic Church. The first chapter includes a church history and applicable background information that is intended to provide an insight into Pope Benedict XVI, the man and the pope. The second chapter provides a picture of Joseph Ratzinger in his early years. Chapter Three covers his studies for the priesthood, and Chapter Four relates his ministry, his obtaining a doctorate degree, and the beginning of his academic life. Chapter Five is the story of his path to Rome and provides the reader with information about his academic career and how he worked closely with Pope John Paul II, whom he met in 1962 at the Second Vatican Council. Chapter Six profiles Benedict XVI as prefect of the CDF; Chapter Seven provides the reader information about his election to the papacy. The last chapter is entitled "The Perspectives of Pope Benedict XVI" and provides information on this pope's prolific writings.

INTRODUCTION

An enormous crowd of pilgrims of all faiths, onlookers, tourists, and the media gathered in and around Saint Peter's Basilica on April 8, 2005, as Pope John Paul II, one of the most beloved popes in history, was carried to his final rest. Just 10 days later, the College of Cardinals convened and Cardinal Bishop Joseph Ratzinger, who had presided over the funeral mass, was elected by the cardinal conclave as the choice for the 265th successor of Saint Peter, taking the name Benedict XVI. His selection, despite his somewhat tenuous health and his age, which would make him the oldest pope since the 18th century, came in rapid consensus. Five days after his election, the new pope said, "When, little by little, the trend of the voting led me to understand that, to say it simply, the axe was going to fall on me, my head began to spin. I was convinced that I had already carried out my life's work and could look forward to ending my days peacefully. With profound conviction I said to the Lord: Do not do this to me! You have younger and better people at your disposal, who can face this great responsibility with greater dynamism and greater strength."[1]

Not long before his election, on the day of his 78th birthday, Cardinal Ratzinger told his co-workers that he was looking forward to his

Saint Peter's Basilica in Vatican City, Rome. (iStockPhoto.com)

retirement and the peace and quiet in his beloved Bavaria. A short time later, he was the leader of the Roman Catholic Church and, according to the Vatican's Statistical Yearbook of the Church, its 1.2 billion members.[2] There were dark clouds hanging over the Church at the time, and being the pontificate, a role he did not seem to expect or necessarily want, would clearly be a difficult, challenging, and certainly a tremendous task and responsibility; it made Benedict XVI realize that it was not God's will for him to find tranquility, but instead, he must allow himself to be led and accept God's will to lead a Church that he had given his life to, and accept the position with a full heart and a stronger-than-ever faith.

The speed of the members of the conclave's selection was significant. Cardinal Ratzinger was chosen within just 24 hours. The swift election shocked some and delighted others within the Church and around the world. The choice was made, in part, on his status for 20 years as the advisor to the Church on doctrinal matters in the important position of Prefect of the Congregation for the Doctrine of the Faith. He was also one of the closest friends and advisors to Pope John Paul II; presiding over the funeral mass for his friend and pope was not an easy task. After all, John Paul II was one of the most beloved popes in all of papal history. As a traditionalist and an intellectual, Benedict XVI as the new pope was elected at a time when many felt the Church needed healing and unifying. Cardinal Ratzinger was a favorite of the traditionalists of the conclave, based on his early academic career that emphasized conservative values and the authority of the Vatican; he was also a well-known theologian. Taking the name Pope Benedict XVI, he identified himself with a religious order that had expanded Christianity in Europe and a name that was consistent with his own hope for a moral revival in an increasingly secular world.

As much as John Paul II was influenced by his Polish roots, so too was Cardinal Ratzinger influenced by his beloved Bavaria; in both cases, their very ancestry significantly shaped them as individuals and as Catholic leaders. Pope Benedict XVI has been described as charming, a man with a resolute faith, and possessing a somewhat shy personal style. He is also someone with an active quick wit and is said to have a great personal kindness, possessing a calm, peaceful spirit with a remarkable ability to listen.

Even though Pope Benedict XVI accepted the difficult challenges confronting the papacy and the Catholic Church worldwide in 2005, and even though he took the office under the banner of continuity with his immensely popular predecessor, this pope, from the beginning of his reign, has been resolute in making his reign very much his own. In his initial encyclical, issued on Christmas 2005, he laid the groundwork by referring to his years of scholarship and to his faith that dates back to his childhood. He said he wanted his words to echo into action—"to call forth in the world . . . a renewed energy and commitment in the human response to God's love."[3]

On April 16, 2012, Pope Benedict XVI celebrated his 85th birthday, making him one of the oldest popes in history. To celebrate his birthday, there were bishops from his native Germany, a German band, and perhaps what was most special—the attendance of his older brother, Georg. In his hometown of Marktl Am Inn, Catholics also celebrated by attending church for a special service to commemorate the pope's birthday. Pope Benedict XVI began his day with a mass where he said,

"I am facing the final leg of the path of my life and I don't know what's ahead. I know though that God's light is there . . . and that his light is stronger than every darkness." Despite his age and continuing health problems, Pope Benedict XVI has ignored rumors of his resignation. Instead, he has "asked for prayers to give [him] strength to fulfill the mission (the Lord) entrusted to me."[4]

George Weigel in the foreword to the book *Light of the World*, a conversation between Peter Seewald and Pope Benedict XVI, notes, "Benedict XVI brought to the papacy more than a half-century of reflection on the truths of biblical faith, and a master teacher's capacity to explicate those truths and bring them to bear on contemporary situations in a luminously clear way."[5] Throughout his life, Benedict XVI has completely given his all to his Church, always guided by his faith. He has led the Roman Catholic Church by maintaining the papacy true to its evangelical origins and the Vatican true to the belief of God. Benedict XVI maintains an eye to the inevitable and eternal challenges to the Catholic Church; yet, he directs it by seeing challenges such as those that are theological, rather than historical. In his years as a theologian, Benedict XVI makes the very substance of the Catholic faith clear, rather than making changes that are not relevant to the Church and its individuals and society as a whole in their changing places and time. To know this pope, there would be no question as to who Pope Benedict XVI is. For those who know him, it is clear that he possesses clarity in his world view and utilizes his sheer force of faith in how he leads the Church. His vision and direction of the Catholic faith may be a challenge to some, and may cause some believers to leave the Church. He is well aware of this. For Benedict XVI, it is always a reminder of the root questions of a religious faith, about the very existence of God, and how God is a part of life that provides the direction of his life and how he leads his flock.

In his years as pontiff, Benedict XVI says he has been sustained by the prayers of people around the world, as he told the pilgrims in Saint Peter's Square during his May 9, 2012, general audience—"From the first moment of my election as the Successor of St. Peter, I have always felt supported by the prayers of you all, by the prayer of the Church, especially by your prayers at moments of greatest difficulty, and I thank you from the bottom of my heart. Unanimous and constant prayer is a precious instrument in overcoming all of the trials that may arise in the path of life, because it is our being deeply united with God that allows us to also be deeply united to others . . . every believer should cultivate a 'constant and trusting' prayer in the Lord, who 'frees us from our chains and guides us.' . . . He gives us serenity of heart to face the difficulties of life, even rejection, opposition and persecution."[6]

NOTES

1. Georg Ratzinger, *My Brother, the Pope* (San Francisco: Ignatius Press, 2011), 232, 233.

2. Cindy Wooden, "Statistically Speaking: Vatican Numbers Hint at Facing Faith Practice," *National Catholic Register*, August 17, 2012, http://ncronline.org.

3. Bart McDowell, *Inside the Vatican* (Washington, DC: National Geographic Society, 1991), 229, 232–233, 238.

4. Nichole Winfield and Daniela Petroff, "Pope Celebrates a Very Bavarian 85th Birthday," *Huffington Post*, April 16, 2012, http://www.huffingtonpost.com.

5. Pope Benedict, *Benedict XVI, Light of the World* (San Francisco: Ignatius Press, 2010), xi.

6. "Pope Reflects on the Power of Prayer," *National Catholic Register*, May 9, 2012, http://www.ncregister.com.

TIMELINE: EVENTS IN THE LIFE OF POPE BENEDICT XVI

April 16, 1927   Joseph Ratzinger is born in Marktl am Inn, Germany, on Holy Saturday, the third and last child of Joseph and Maria Ratzinger.

1927   The family moves to Tittmoning on the Austrian border; in 1932, they move again, to Auschau am Inn, at the foot of the Alps.

1933   Adolf Hitler is elected as German chancellor.

1937   Admitted to the *Gymnasium* (secondary school) in Traunstein, Germany, and begins his study of classical languages (Latin and Greek).

1939   Enters Saint Michael Seminary, the archdiocesan minor seminary in Traunstein.

1941   Required to enroll in the Nazi Youth while at seminary.

1943–1945   Drafted as helper for antiaircraft defense unit, and later an infantry soldier; in 1944, he is released from his unit and returns home; later, he is drafted to serve in a labor detail on the border area with Hungary; upon his release, he returns home, and after three weeks, is drafted into the German infantry at Munich and serves in various posts around Traunstein.

1945 Leaves the Army post and returns home; when the Americans arrive and occupy the village, he is identified as a soldier and, in May–June, is imprisoned at an American P.O.W. camp.

In November, begins studies for the priesthood in Freising, Germany.

1946–1951 Studies philosophy and theology at the College for Philosophy and Theology in Freising, near Munich, followed by studies in theology at the University of Munich; completes post-graduate work in Freising while preparing for priestly ordination.

1951 On June 29, ordained as Roman Catholic priest, along with his older brother, Georg. Is assigned to Saint Martin's Parish as the assistant priest, and later is a chaplain at the Precious Blood Parish in Munich.

1952–1954 Serves as an instructor at the major seminary in Freising while assisting at the churches in Freising.

1953 In July, receives doctorate in theology from the University of Munich.

1954–1955 Serves as instructor for dogmatic and fundamental theology at the College of Philosophy in Freising.

1957 Completes his *Habilitation* (post-doctoral dissertation) at the University of Munich in the department of fundamental theology.

1958–1959 Is professor for dogmatic and fundamental theology in Freising.

1959–1963 Is professor for fundamental theology at the University of Bonn.

1962–1965 Is an advisor to Cardinal Joseph Frings of Cologne and official councilor theologian at Vatican II; also serves as a member of the Doctrinal Committee of the German Bishops and of the International Pontifical Theological Commission in Rome.

1963–1966 Is professor for dogmatics and the history of dogma at the University of Münster.

1966–1969 Is the Chair in dogmatic theology at University of Tübingen.

1969–1977 Is professor for dogmatics and the history of dogma, and later, is vice president at the University of Regensburg; with Hans Urs von Balthasar, Henri de Lubac, and others, founds the International Catholic Journal *Communio*.

1970 Builds a home near Regensburg to be his retreat and his family's gathering place.

1977 On March 14, is appointed Archbishop of Munich and Freising by Pope Paul VI; two months later, is consecrated as bishop.

1977 On June 27, receives red hat of a cardinal and is appointed cardinal-priest of S. Maria Consolatrice al Tiburtino.

1978 In August, in the year of three popes, after the death of Paul VI, participates in the conclave that elects Pope John Paul I, who died in September; then participates in the conclave to elect Cardinal Karol Wojtyla, the Archbishop of Krakow, who takes the name Pope John Paul II.

1980 Declines Pope John Paul II's invitation to head the Congregation for Catholic Education in the Roman curia.

1981 On November 25, is appointed prefect of the Congregation for the Doctrine of the Faith (CDF) and thereby also appointed the President of Pontifical Biblical Commission and the International Theological Commission by Pope John Paul II.

1982 Resigns as Archbishop of Munich and Freising.

1986–1992 Serves as Head of the Pontifical Commission for the preparation of the *Catechism of the Catholic Church*, presented in December 1992; in 1991, is a member of the European Academy of Arts and Sciences; in

1992, elected member of the Académie des sciences morales et politiques of the Institut de Frances, Paris.

1993 On April 5, is appointed cardinal-bishop of Velletri-Segni.

2002 On November 30, is appointed cardinal-bishop of Ostia and becomes dean of the College of Cardinals.

2005 On April 2, on the death of Pope John Paul II, resigns as prefect of the Doctrine of the Faith, as president of the International Theological Commission, and as president of the Pontifical Biblical Commission, Roman curia.

On April 8, officiates at Pope John Paul II's funeral.

On April 18, it is the beginning of the conclave to elect a new pope, as 115 of the cardinals that are eligible to vote enter the Sistine Chapel; he gives the opening address on "relativism."

On April 19, in a relatively short, 26-hour conclave, is elected bishop of Rome, the 265th pope in the history of the Catholic Church, by his fellow cardinals on the fourth ballot of the conclave; takes the name Benedict XVI.

On April 21, announces an email address: benedictxvi@vatican.va.

On April 24, is formally installed as pope.

On May 9, opens the beatification process for John Paul II.

In August, makes an apostolic visit to Cologne, Germany, on the occasion of the 20th World Youth Day.

In September, grants a television interview—the first ever for a Pope—to the Polish network TVP.

In October, takes part in the discussions of the regular General Assembly of the 11th World Synod of Bishops.

In December, delivers his first encyclical entitled *Deus caritas est*, "God is Love," in which he describes love as the central dimension of Christianity.

2006   In March, begins to downsize the curia by merging
       pontifical councils and begins to assign multiple du-
       ties to individual bishops.

       In May, visits Poland.

       In July, visits Spain for the Fifth World Family
       Conference.

       In September, visits his birthplace in Bavaria, Mu-
       nich, Regensburg, and Freising, Germany.

       In October, visits Verona, Italy.

       In November, visits Turkey.

       In December, meets with the Israeli prime minister
       and the Coptic Patriarch.

2007   In January, meets with the prime minister of Viet-
       nam, the first visit of a Vietnamese head of govern-
       ment to the Vatican since the Communist seizure of
       power in 1975.

       In March, meets with the Russian president Vladimir
       Putin.

       In March, meets with the general secretary of the
       United Nations.

       In April, volume one of his book *Jesus of Nazareth* is
       published on his 80th birthday; also visits Vigevano,
       in the Lombardy region of Italy, and makes a pil-
       grimage to the tomb of Saint Augustine.

       In May, visits Brazil; his book *Jesus of Nazareth* is
       published in the United States.

       In June, receives President George W. Bush at the
       Vatican.

       In September, visits Loreto, Italy; meets with the
       Israeli prime minister; visits Austria; visits Velletri
       and Naples, Italy.

       In November, meets with the King Abdullah of
       Saudi Arabia, the first audience of a Saudi monarch
       with the leader of the Catholic Church.

2008   In April, visits the United States and is received at
       the White House on his 81st birthday; meets with

sex abuse victims in Boston; addresses the United Nations General Assembly, visits Ground Zero in New York City, and celebrates mass at baseball's Nationals Park and Yankee Stadium.

In May, meets with a delegation of Shiite Muslims from Iran; meets with the Primate of the Anglicans, Archbishop Rowan Williams of Canterbury; visits Savona and Genoa, Italy.

In June, meets with U.S. president George W. Bush.

In July, visits Sydney, Australia.

In September, visits Lourdes, France.

2009 In January, is listed in *Newsweek* magazine as Number 37 on the list of the world's most influential people.

In January, launches a Vatican channel on YouTube.

In February, meets with leaders of the Conference of Presidents of Major American Jewish Organizations and condemns anti-Semitism and rejects any denial of the Holocaust.

In March, travels to the countries of Cameroon and Angola.

In May, visits the Holy Land, Jordan, Israel, and the Palestinian territories; visits the Holocaust Memorial Yad Vashem in Jerusalem; is the first pope to visit the Muslim Dome of the Rock on the Temple Mount; prays at the Wailing Wall and visits the Church of the Holy Sepulcher in Jerusalem.

In June, proclaims the beginning of the "Year for Priests."

In July, receives President Barack Obama at the Vatican; meets with the Australian prime minister; meets with the South Korean president.

In September, visits the Czech Republic.

2010 In February, meets with Irish bishops to address the abuse scandal in the Catholic Church of Ireland.

In April, visits Malta to mark the occasion of the landing of the Apostle Paul on the island 1,950 years ago.

In May, visits Portugal.

In September, visits the United Kingdom, the first State visit by a pope; meets with Queen Elizabeth II, the head of the Anglican Church, in Edinburgh.

In November, his book *Light of the World* is published and in November, he issues a warning to internet users that the Web has "numbed" young people and has created an "educational" emergency; visits Spain.

2011   In January, weighs in on social media, telling Catholic bloggers and users of Facebook and YouTube to be respectful of others when spreading the gospel online.

In May, the NBC network's *Today* show broadcasts live from the Vatican; in May, speaks via satellite with astronauts aboard the International Space Station, making it the first time a pope has conversed with astronauts in space.

In June, meets privately with Vice President Joe Biden at the Vatican.

In August, visits Madrid for World Youth Day.

In September, calls for a common front with Orthodox Christians to defend traditional church values on a four-day official visit to Germany.

In October, prays at the crypt at Saint Francis in Assisi, Italy.

In November, visits Africa.

2012   In January, the Vatican is shaken by a corruption scandal after an Italian television investigation said a former top Vatican official had been transferred against his will after complaining about irregularities in awarding contracts.

In January, names 22 cardinals.

In February, begins sending out tweets on Twitter as daily messages during Lent.

In March, visits Mexico; visits Cuba, a visit coinciding with the 400th anniversary of the patron saint.

In April, the Vatican announces a doctrinal crackdown on the leadership organization representing most of the 57,000 nuns in the United States, over social justice issues and women ordination.

In April, celebrates his 85th birthday.

In May, his personal butler, Paolo Gabriele, is arrested for allegedly having confidential documents in his home.

In May, breaks his silence over the leaked documents scandal, saying he was saddened by the betrayal and was grateful for the aides who work faithfully and in silence to help him do his job.

In May, expresses his gratitude to American nuns for their self-sacrifice and praises U.S. bishops for their efforts to welcome immigrants.

In June, celebrates an open-air mass for a million pilgrims at World Meeting of Families in Milan, Italy.

In June, announces visit to Philadelphia in 2015 for the Church's triennial World Meeting of Families.

In October, names seven new saints, including two Americans.

2013   On February 11, announces he will step down as pope to be effective on February 28, 2013, at 8:00 p.m., Rome time.

Chapter 1

AN INTRODUCTION TO THE VATICAN AND TO THE POPES OF THE MODERN ERA

On April 19, 2005, just three days after his 78th birthday, Cardinal Joseph Ratzinger became the 265th successor of Saint Peter and the leader of the Catholic Church, and the wearer of the shoes of the fisherman. The new pope, taking the name Benedict XVI, determined that he would not be the prince of the Church, but rather a servant of the Church. Early in his life, he chose the Church and dedicated his life to its service. His very being is profoundly and absolutely steeped in the deep and lasting traditions of the Catholic Church; he completely and utterly exhausts himself in his giving wholeheartedly to the Church and to his flock of Catholics, estimated to be nearly 1.2 billion, according to the Vatican's Statistical Yearbook of the Church.[1]

To understand the life of Benedict XVI, to read his words, to understand his directives, and to discern what he profoundly believes, it is important to understand how and why he is called "the great giver" and the absolute leader of the Catholic Church. In any biography of a pope, and certainly in the story of this pope, it is important to understand the role of the Vatican, the Holy See, and the popes who came before him, especially those of the 20th century, known as the modern era of popes of the Catholic Church. Without a doubt, as one who is on the throne, the leader of the Catholic Church has an exceptional view of the world. A biography of any pope would not be complete without knowledge of the history of the Church and the Vatican. In addition, all popes throughout history are seen both individually and through their service to the church—from their personal beliefs, to what shaped their papacy, and how each pope lived, directed the Church, and died as a servant of the Church. The long, varied, and sometimes violent history of the Catholic Church has intrinsically influenced all those who have occupied the Chair of Saint Peter. Certainly, all of this has influenced the life and service of Pope Benedict XVI.

THE VATICAN

For many throughout the world, it is a place like no other. The Vatican, officially the State of Vatican City, is the territorial base of the Holy See. To Roman Catholics, the Holy See is primarily the diocese of Rome, presided over by its bishop, the pope. It is also the central government of the Church.

According to Bart McDowell, author of *Inside the Vatican*, the Vatican city-state was established as a result of the Lateran Agreements signed on February 11, 1929, between the Holy See and the Italian government. The Vatican is an enclave within the city of Rome, Italy, and is the smallest country in existence, with an area of just 110 acres, on which there are buildings, roads, and gardens. The basilica at the Vatican is the largest church in the world. The United Nations declared the Vatican a World Heritage site for its extraordinary cultural importance, which entitles it to special protection. Author McDowell writes, "In the eyes of church officials, the primary purpose of the Vatican State is to provide political independence to the pope as head of the Catholic Church. As an independent sovereign, the pope is subject to no government or political power." The Vatican has no privately owned real estate, no income taxes, and no general elections. For a comparative perspective, the Vatican is smaller than the grounds of the U.S. Capitol in Washington, D.C., is about one-fourth the size of the country Monaco, and is one-eighth as big as New York City's Central Park.[2]

According to the official website, the Vatican: the Holy See, accessed at http://www.vaticanstate.va, "The population of Vatican

City is about 800 people, of whom over 450 have Vatican citizenship, while the rest have permission to reside there, either temporarily or permanently, without the benefit of citizenship. About half of the Vatican's citizens do not live inside Vatican City. Because of their occupations (mostly as diplomatic personnel), they live in different countries around the world. The conferral or loss of citizenship, authorization to live inside Vatican City and formalities for entering the territory is governed by special regulations issued according to the Lateran Treaty." The Vatican is surrounded by walls and stretches into Saint Peter's Square, marking the boundary of the state and the edge of the square, which is normally open to everyone. There are five entrances to Vatican City, "each of them guarded by the Pontifical Swiss Guards and by the Gendarmes Corps of Vatican City State. The entrance to the Vatican Museums is on *Viale Vatican*, not far from *Piazza del Risorgimento*. Because Vatican City is so small, several departments and offices belonging to the Holy See are situated in buildings around Rome (in *Piazza Pio XII*, *Via della Conciliazione*, *Piazza San Calisto*, *Piazza della Cancelleria and in Piazza di Spagna*). According to

The Swiss Guards of Vatican City, Rome. (Shutterstock)

the Lateran Treaty, these buildings enjoy the same status, recognized by international law, as embassies and foreign diplomatic missions abroad. The areas occupied by these buildings are commonly known as 'extraterritorial.'"[3]

The Vatican City has its own post office and a radio station that dates back to 1931, when it was used to broadcast the pope's messages to the world. The Vatican library is one of the world's greatest repositories of medieval and Renaissance manuscripts and incunabula, which are books printed prior to 1501. The Vatican also is the repository of the archives whose primary purpose is to maintain the popes' records and files. Quite possibly, the most famous treasure of the Vatican is the Sistine Chapel, painted by Michelangelo. The Chapel is still among the most visited sites in Rome today. The Vatican also holds a vast art collection that includes the paintings and sculptures in its gardens and museums, including one of the most viewed art works located inside Saint Peter's Basilica—Michelangelo's famous "Pietá," a grieving Virgin Mary holding her dead son. Viewers speak softly as they view the masterpiece, and some kneel and pray.

Visitors of the Vatican City are not allowed to wander about alone. Visitors must sign up for an escorted tour of the gardens and are able to purchase a ticket for the museums and see the wonders of the Vatican, including the Sistine Chapel. All visitors are under the watchful eye of Swiss Guards who have sworn their allegiance to the pope. These guards become citizens of the Vatican during their term of service to the Vatican. Volunteers of the Guard must be veterans of the Swiss Army and must be between the ages of 19 and 30 years when they begin a two-year tour of duty. They must also be Catholic, unmarried, and be "of good family." The Swiss Guards are charged with protecting the pope and his properties; their service dates from 1506.

HOW POPES ARE ELECTED

The Roman Catholic Church, from its earliest days, has held that the leader of the Church is the pope. The first pope, Saint Peter the Apostle, reigned as pope during AD 33–AD 67. Catholics believe that the pope is a direct successor of Saint Peter, and that the pope is Christ's representative on earth. Roman Catholics believe, however, that he is not selected by divine intervention; rather, he is elected as a result of a secret vote in a conclave where the electors—the Catholic cardinals who have not yet reached the age of 80 on the day the papacy becomes vacant—meet to vote and to elect a new pope. When a pope dies, the cardinals gather in secret to pray for guidance and to vote, based on their beliefs of who, from the circle of cardinals, is best suited to serve as pope, based on the church's mission and imperatives at the time, and based on who is deemed as the most qualified to preside over the Church. There are times when certain cardinals may be the best qualified; however, based on political biases, they are not elected. As in votes for political leaders around the world, there is often the making of promises that benefit one cardinal or a group of cardinals, and their vote is the vote that elects the pope.

Because Catholic doctrine dictates that the pope is the bishop of Rome and is the successor of Saint Peter and the vicar of Christ on earth, the process for electing a pope is often difficult, significant, and more often than not, is a time-consuming process. Cardinals might oppose one candidate and lobby for their own preferred candidate. Those whose name is put forth for deliberation often compete with one another, and sometimes a cardinal may not want his name put forth for consideration. There is competition and there is compromise. Even though the meeting is held in conclave, in private, what is happening in the outside world at the time is always considered by the electors who come from around the world. Events in their own countries and around the world are important and also a part of the deliberations and final election process. In addition, because there are humans involved in the election process, there is also the quest for power; there is also greed, self-interest, and individual political beliefs that are often involved in this important process. Personal, human, and spiritual considerations are a part of the process when an individual cardinal votes for a new pope who will go on to lead the Catholic Church.

For the first 1,000 years of the Catholic Church, popes were elected by the people and the clergy of Rome because the pope was the bishop of the local church, or the diocese of Rome. By the fourth and fifth centuries, while this same process continued, the influence widened to include bishops from the surrounding dioceses; and later, the clergy, bishops, and influential laypersons, including military officials, were prominent in decisions, even more so than that of ordinary citizens, in the election of the bishop of Rome. For years, the levels of political beliefs and personal biases had become increasingly important. By the 10th century, the aristocratic families of Rome overwhelmed the voices of the laity and the clergy. The aristocrats ruled the city of Rome as well as the papacy. During the 11th century, it was the German kings who controlled the papacy, with the election of four consecutive German popes; and after the Germans, it was a French pope, Nicholas II, who decreed that the election of the pope would be by the votes of cardinals and bishops, and not by bribery and promises, as had been the case for many years.

Throughout the years, from the 11th century until the election of Pope John Paul II in 1978, the election of popes was often chaotic and the rules governing the elections changed many times. In 1996, Pope John Paul II changed the process to require a majority of two-thirds vote; it was then possible for a candidate to be elected pope by a simple majority if a candidate still has not received the necessary two-thirds majority. In 1970, Pope John Paul II decreed that only cardinals under the age of 80 were eligible to vote in papal elections, with the maximum number of cardinal-electors set at 120.[4]

There is no provision in the Catholic Church's Code of Canon Law for the removal of a pope. A pope either dies or resigns, a vacancy is created, and a new pope is elected. There is also no provision where a pope may become mentally incompetent, become critically ill and cannot serve, or suffer from a disability that prevents him from serving as pope; there is no provision where the pope may be deemed to be heretical—a situation where the pope holds an opinion or belief that contradicts the established teachings of the Catholic Church, and should be removed from office. Canon law puts forth and assumes that as pope, he is, and always will be until death, the supreme leader of the Church. The same Canon law makes clear that "there is neither appeal nor recourse against a decision or decree of the Roman Pontiff" and "one who takes recourse against an act of the Roman Pontiff to an ecumenical council or to the college of bishops is to be punished with a censure."[5] The pope is considered the absolute monarch of the Catholic Church.

THE MODERN POPES—FROM SAINT PIUS X TO POPE JOHN PAUL II

By the end of the 19th century, the Vatican's wealth was at an all-time low. In compensation, however, the pope's spiritual role and emblematic power remained very high and the pope was the revered spiritual leader throughout the world, the unquestioned head of the largest Christian Church. Prior to this time, popes typically used their power to denounce secular thought. However, at the beginning of the 20th century, the papacy was tested many times and as never before. In this new era, there were waves of new thoughts in philosophy, in the sciences, in the study of history, and in biblical criticism. Changes of thoughts were prominent in societies and governments throughout the world. In addition, the world was seeing the rise of evil dictatorships, including the rise of the Nazis and Hitler in Germany and of Stalin in Russia. The pope and the Vatican's response to prevailing questions and changes of thought within the Church and the rise of evil and savagery in the world tested the papacy and the Church itself.

THE MODERN POPES, BEGINNING WITH SAINT PIUS X (1835–1914), WHO SERVED AS POPE DURING 1903–1914

Saint Pius X was elected as the 255th pope in 1903. From his death in 1914 through to Pope John Paul II's election in 1978, there have been just eight popes. Saint Pius X, born Giuseppe Sarto, was ordained in the Church in 1858 and worked for the first eight years as a country curate, or an assistant to a priest; over the next nine years, he was a parish priest, and in 1875, he was named chancellor of his home diocese of Treviso, Italy, and the spiritual director of its major seminary. In 1884, he was appointed bishop, and in 1893, he was named patriarch of Venice and a cardinal. As Cardinal Sarto, he was elected pope on August 4, 1903. Upon his election, it seemed that he was chosen because he was completely different from the previous pope, Leo XIII, a pope considered to be remote in his rule, and regal in his outlook. It was French cardinal Mathieu who later said, "We wanted a pope who had never engaged in politics, whose name would signify peace and concord, who had grown old in the care of souls, who would concern himself with the government of the Church in detail, who would be above all a father and a shepherd."[6] While this was the prevailing feeling among some, there were others within the Vatican curia, the administrative body of the Vatican, who wanted the policies of Leo XIII, whose political reign lasted from 1878 to 1903, to continue. While Leo XIII was considered to be austere, detached, and very politically astute, Pius X was strong emotionally, with piety and humanity at his core.

There were a number of important changes during Pius X's reign as pope—a simplification of the Code of Cannon Law, changes to how priests were educated, and of how catechism was taught in parishes. He also reformed the Church's prayer life through the Catholic prayer book and the missal, a book that contains prayers, responses to prayers, and the hymns used during the Catholic mass. Pope Pius X also waged a campaign to get parishioners to receive communion more regularly. He is also remembered as the pope who lowered the age of the first communion to what was known as the age of discretion, or approximately, seven. All of these changes, some small, but all memorable, were prevalent during the Second Vatican Council that took place during 1962–1965.[7]

In 1913, Pope Pius X suffered a heart attack, which left him diminished in strength. He was also very disheartened about the events that led to World War I, especially the assassination of Archduke Francis Ferdinand, the heir to the Austrian–Hungarian throne in June 1914. Pius X died on August 20, 1914, and was buried in a simple tomb in a crypt at Saint Peter's, which was in accordance to his wishes. He was known as a Pope of the People and his reign set in motion many influences of the popes in the modern era. In 1923, the process for his canonization began, and on May 29, 1954, he was canonized a saint and became known as Saint Pius X.

Pope Benedict XV (1854–1922), Served as Pope during 1914–1922

Pope Benedict XV was the 256th pope and was elected on September 3, 1914, upon the death of Pope Pius X. Born Giacomo della Chiesa, his nickname in seminary was *Piccoletto*, which meant "tiny." Born to aristocratic parents in Genoa, della Chiesa, he had a shoulder, an eye and an ear each higher than the other, due to an injury at birth. He was also stoop-shouldered, had a bluish tinge to his complexion, and walked with a decided limp. When he was elected pope in 1914, none of the papal robes kept in readiness for the election were small enough to fit him.

Della Chiesa was ordained in 1878 and then studied at what is now known as the Pontifical Ecclesiastical Academy, a training school for Vatican diplomats in Rome. From 1883 to 1887, della Chiesa served as secretary to Archbishop Mariano Rampolla. When Rampolla was named cardinal secretary of state to then Pope Leo XII in 1901, della Chiesa was named the undersecretary. Pope Pius X appointed him as the archbishop of Bologna in 1907. In May 1914, della Chiesa was appointed cardinal and took his new post at the Vatican. By that time, the pope was seriously ill and soon died. Just three months later, on September 3, 1914, della Chiesa was elected pope, taking the name Benedict XV. His election came as a surprise since he had so recently been named cardinal. His diplomatic experience was likely to have been one consideration by the conclave in light of the breakout of World War I just a month prior to the election.

It was the war that dominated Benedict XV's term as pope. Known as a compassionate priest, he used his office from the very first days of his reign to distribute as much of the Vatican's money as possible to those in need and he continually sought ways to ease the suffering caused by the war. He attempted to reunite prisoners with their families and persuaded Switzerland to accept soldiers from any country that suffered from tuberculosis. He also strove to use his diplomatic skills to find solutions to end the war. Throughout, he was determined to remain neutral, believing that the Holy See would be listened to and remain credible if neutrality was maintained. Unfortunately, this stance caused both sides of the conflict to suspect Benedict XV and the Vatican of partiality and of favoring the other side. Benedict XV continued to refuse to condemn any side and continually sought solutions for a negotiated peace. In August 1917, he proposed a peace plan that included the return of all occupied territories, which was ignored. As the Armistice was reached in 1919, to his own great disappointment, Benedict XV was excluded from the negotiations. His monetary contributions in service to the poor and to the wounded and displaced people as a result of the war were remembered; however, as a result, the Vatican coffers were empty.

After the war, Benedict XV used his diplomatic skills to further reconciliation. The aftermath of the long war left much of the political structure within Europe in chaos and Benedict XV endeavored to secure the position of the Catholic Church and the Vatican throughout France, Russian, Spain, and the Balkans by sending his emissaries on missions. Within the Church, Benedict XV encouraged Catholics to join the trade union movements; he also initiated reconciliation with France, and canonized Joan of Arc in 1920. In 1922, Benedict XV had increased the papacy's diplomatic standing throughout Europe. Pope Benedict XV died at the age of 67 of complications of influenza on January 22, 1922. He was buried in a crypt at Saint Peter's Basilica.

Pope Pius XI (1857–1939),
Served as Pope during 1922–1939

As the first pope to use the radio to communicate to his followers, and the first to have an enthusiastic love of mountaineering, Pope Pius XI was elected pope on February 6, 1922. He was also the pope who established the Vatican city-state as a separate and independent political entity, after discussions with the Italian dictator Benito Mussolini. Born Ambrogio Damiano achille Ratti, Pius XI was a scholar who spent most of his working life as a librarian, first at Ambrosiano, in his native Milan, and then at the Vatican. Ratti was a gifted linguist, with his German and French linguistic proficiency extremely useful in his work prior to his election as pope. Ratti earned three doctorate degrees, was a seminary professor, and worked at the Ambrosian Library in Milan. In 1911, he was appointed to the Vatican Library and was made prefect, or senior administrator, in 1914. On February 6, 1922, Ratti was elected pope, taking the name Pius XI in honor of Pius IX, who had supported him in his early years, and also in honor of Pius X, who had called him to Rome for service at the Vatican Library. His election had not come easy, being elected on the 14th ballot.

Pope Pius XI's first act was one of reconciliation between the Vatican and the Italian state. He gave his first pontifical blessing from the external balcony of Saint Peter's Basilica, the first time since 1870.

He took as his motto "Christ's peace in Christ's kingdom," making the point that the Church should be active in the world and not isolated from it.[8] Pius XI also took a keen interest in mission work and instructed every religious order to complete missionary work. He consecrated the first native Chinese bishops in 1926, as well as a native Japanese bishop in 1927. In 1933, he ordained priests from India, Southeast Asia, and China. As a result of his dedication to missionary work, the number of native priests in missions increased from nearly 3,000 to more than 7,000. In addition, the number of Catholics in China rose from 9 million to 21 million.[9] Pius XI's papacy was not without its political difficulties, despite his stance for reconciliation. Having been elected in post–World War I Europe, his papacy also extended into the years just prior to World War II, in a world of fascism in Italy and in Nazi Germany. One of his most important political initiatives was in 1929, with the Lateran Treaty, reached with the Italian prime minister Benito Mussolini, after more than two years of difficult negotiations. This agreement allowed for the independent sovereign state known as the Vatican City. Pius XI had already established the Church's own post office and radio station, which allowed for the freedom of communication with the world, and allowed Pius XI—the first pope to do so—to use this medium as a means of pastoral communication. The treaty also allowed for the recognition of canon law alongside the law of the state, giving the Church control over Catholic marriages, and made religious instruction in secondary schools and the teachings of Catholic doctrine in state schools mandatory, and also allowed for the fixation of the crucifix in classrooms; it also gave the Vatican significant financial compensation from the Italian government. In all, some 20 concordats and other agreements were concluded. From his attention to agreements in Italy and other European countries, Pius XI turned his attention to Germany and Russia. In his condemnation of communism in 1933, Pius XI entered into a concordat with Germany's Nazi government; Pius XI trusted Hitler's assurances that the rights of the Catholic Church would be respected. However, all it did was accord respect to the Hitler regime. Pius XI, between 1933 and 1936, communicated with the Nazi government to protest against its growing oppression of the Catholic Church in Germany; however, most of his letters went unanswered. In 1937, Pope Pius XI issued an encyclical, or formal statement, which denounced the violations of the agreement signed in 1933, and condemned Nazism as fundamentally racist and anti-Christian. This encyclical was to be read from every German pulpit. Nazi government officials were furious and intensified their persecution of the Church and its priests. Meanwhile, the Italian government adopted Hitler's racist doctrines, and in 1938, a rupture occurred between the Vatican and Mussolini's government. Pius XI issued an encyclical critical of Italian fascism.[10]

Pope Pius XI was considered to be authoritarian in his exercise of papal ministry. To the end, he strived to denounce fascism, to make known his absolute loathing of communism, and his total repudiation of the tyrannies happening in Germany; he stated that no Christian could be anti-Semitic. In the last years of his life, he ceased to be the diplomat and became somewhat of a prophet. He was known to have championed the religious freedoms of all people. Upon his death on February 10, 1939, the British government's correspondent in Rome, D'Arcy Osborne, who was not always an admirer of the pope, wrote that "Pius' courage at the end of his life had ensured that he became 'one of the outstanding figures of the world,' and that 'he may be said to have died at his post.'"[11]

Pius XII (1876–1958),
Served as Pope during 1939–1958

For Eugenio Pacelli, the election as pope came on the first day of the conclave in March 1939. His unusually quick election was because he was seemingly the inevitable choice. He was thought to be a skilled political diplomat and had been groomed to succeed Pius XI, who had dispatched him all over the world as nuncio, or the ambassador of the pope.

Born Eugenio Maria Giuseppe Giovanni Pacelli, he came to possess a natural seriousness and an intense devotion to the Catholic faith. As pope, he was known to pray during the night in the crypts of his predecessors, and in photographs, he was typically seen to be poised in prayer.

While his predecessor served as pope in post–World War I until just prior to the outbreak of World War II, Cardinal Pacelli was elected pope and became Pope Pius XII in a time of war, a time when all of his attributes would be required—from his ease in diplomacy, to his language skills, and to his travels throughout Europe as an emissary of Pius XI. He was sent to Germany, where he served as nuncio for many years, and spoke fluent German. Despite serving in Germany and his affection for the people, the culture, and music, he was known to condemn Nazi policies and their inherent racism. He believed that Soviet communism, rather than fascism and Nazism, was the enemy. With all his beliefs as pope, the World War II Allies viewed him with suspicion because he was seen to be pro-Italian and pro-German. He was, however, deeply committed to his role as the spiritual leader of all nations and of world peace; he spent his first months as pope attempting to prevent yet another world war. He declared in August 1939, "Nothing is lost by peace: everything may be lost by war."[12] He also undertook a radio address in August 1940 to appeal to the world on behalf of peace.

Once war broke out, he struggled with the expectation of taking sides, and tried in vain to promote peace and prevent the ongoing atrocities and inhumanity. Hoping to obtain a negotiated peace agreement, and realizing this was not possible while Hitler reigned, in 1940, he acted as an intermediary between the Allies and a group of army conspirators who planned to assassinate Hitler. His role in this effort was kept secret, believing he was acting immorally. Despite all of his efforts, he began to weigh everything and as a result, became more and more indecisive. This became evident on the question of the Nazi's genocide against the Jews, and as the war continued, Pius XII was under pressure to speak out against the genocide and the Nazi atrocities. The Allies hoped to use his denunciation in the effort to win the war; the pope's advisors wanted him to speak out to clearly express the Church's stance, and he refused to do so. He believed it would do nothing to help the Jews and would cause even more persecution of the Catholics by the Nazis. However, he did direct the Vatican to use Vatican funds to help the Jews, paid a ransom demanded for the safety of Roman Jews, and as pressure by the Italian Jewish community mounted, he opened religious houses as places of refuge.

In 1942, Pius' Christmas message to the Catholics included what he believed to be a clear denunciation of the Jewish genocide. He asked that all men of goodwill bring society back to the rule of God, declaring it a duty "we owe to the war dead, to their mothers, their

widows and orphans, to those exiled by war, and to the 'hundreds
of thousands of innocent people put to death or doomed to slow ex-
tinction, sometimes merely because of their race or their descent.'"[13]
The speech was not received well by Mussolini or by Nazi Germany;
the pope, they believed, had abandoned his stance as neutral and had
unequivocally condemned the Nazi actions against the Jews. The Allies, conversely, believed the speech was a feeble attempt to condemn
the obvious atrocities. After the war, the Vatican undertook immense
efforts to assist in finding the millions of missing persons; however,
after all the humanitarian efforts, both during and after the war by the
pope and the Vatican, controversies over whether Pius XII was anti-
Semitic continued, despite him being vigorously defended by those
surrounding him. He was severely criticized for his failure to speak out
and to act more forcefully on behalf of the Jews. The Vatican took a
bold step in forming a committee of historians to publish everything
connected to the Vatican's involvement with the war and what was
known as the Jewish question. What followed were 11 volumes of
documents that denounced the specific allegations of what the Vatican and Pope Pius XII did and did not do during the war. Many who
have taken the view of the pope's positions during the war, and his not
clearly denouncing the Nazi genocide of the Jews, speculate that his
experience as the named diplomat by the Vatican to Germany in the
1920s, his partiality to Germans and German culture, and his hatred
of communism and it being more dangerous than Nazism had much
to do with his reluctance to speak out when he was pressured to do so
at the time.

Despite this pope's public positions on the Holocaust that dominated his papacy, he was very instrumental in carrying out many pastoral and religious activities. There were few moral or religious topics
that he did not touch upon in his pronouncements. He canonized 33
persons during his papacy, including Pius X, and consecrated a large
number of cardinals from many countries around the world. Due to the
relatively new prevalence of radio, newsreels, and later on, television,
this pope became the best known leader of the Catholic people at that
time. Pope Pius XII died at Castel Gandolfo, the summer residence for
the pope, on October 9, 1958. By that time, he had gained considerable
credibility and influence during his reign as pope within the Catholic

Church and among non-Catholics too throughout the world. He was buried in Saint Peter's Basilica.

Pope John XXIII (1881–1963), Served as Pope during 1958–1963

When Pope Pius XII died in 1958, he had served as pope since 1939. The conclave was divided on how to replace him after such a long period. There were some who were committed to extending Pius XII's policies, and another group of younger cardinals who wanted changes. As a result of the deadlock, the conclave looked for an interim pope and their choice was the 77-year-old Patriarch of Venice, known as a genial diplomat, who had been named Patriarch on his retirement. It was felt he would not make many changes and everyone believed that as a result of his age, it would give the Vatican time to choose a younger and more vigorous man to set the Church's agenda.

Born Angelo Giuseppe Roncalli, he was the third of 13 children in a family of peasant farmers. Ordained in 1904, he was named secretary to his bishop in Bergamo, Italy, and was a lecturer of church history. During World War I, he served as a hospital orderly, and later, a military chaplain. It was Pope Pius XI, who served as pope during 1922–1939, who launched Father Roncalli on his diplomatic career; the latter served in Greece, Bulgaria, and Turkey. During the German occupation of Greece from 1941 to 1944, Father Roncalli did all that was in his power to relieve the distress of the people, and in particular, in preventing the deportation of Jews. In 1944, he was appointed as nuncio to France, where he had to deal with the reputation of bishops thought to have collaborated with the pro-Nazi Vichy regime. He was also the Vatican's first permanent observer at the United Nations Educational, Scientific, and Cultural Organization (UNESCO), in 1951 and 1952. In 1953, Father Roncalli was named cardinal and the Patriarch of Venice. With all his diplomatic experience and despite his humble origins, he was considered to be highly cultured; he was prolific in French, Bulgarian, Russian, Turkish, and modern Greek.

When Father Roncalli was elected pope, after 11 ballots, he took the name John XXIII for several reasons. It was his father's name; it was the name of the church where he was baptized, and also the name of numerous cathedrals around the world, including the pope's own cathedral, Saint John Lateran. He also took the name because he said it was the name of the two men closest to Jesus—John the Baptist and John the Evangelist. When he gave his first papal blessing from the balcony of Saint Peter's Basilica, it was, for the first time in history, televised. At his coronation on November 4, 1958, he said he wanted to be a good shepherd and he reminded the congregation of Saint John Lateran that he was "a priest, a father, a shepherd."[14] As pope, he visited prisoners at a local jail as well as local parishes, hospitals, convalescent homes for the elderly, and other educational and charitable institutions.

Of all his accomplishments during his short time as pope, John XXIII has been considered by some to be an outstanding pope. He called for the Second Vatican Council and set the Catholic Church on a new course, where he emphasized the role of the Church laity—those followers who are not Church clergy—for collegiality, or shared equal power of Church bishops, and the recognized faith of non-Catholic Christians and non-Christians, and the absolute dignity of all human beings. Throughout his papacy, John XXIII issued his encyclicals, or his own formal statements, which reflected his pastoral and ecumenical tone. The June 1959 theme was of truth, unity, and peace, and noted non-Catholics as brethren. His May 1961 encyclical noted the rights of workers and the obligations of governments. The April 1963 encyclical, published less than two months before his death, insisted that the recognition of human rights and responsibilities is the foundation for world peace.[15]

Pope John XXIII was committed to Christian unity. He made his last public appearance from the window of his apartment in the Vatican on May 23, 1963. He said a prayer in his musical, strong voice and the applause was so strong, he was almost prevented from giving his blessing. The next few days were filled with pain from cancer for Pope John XXIII; yet, he was able to make statements about the global human community, and he continued to pray for unity, not only of the Church, but of all humans. He said, "It is not that the gospel has changed, it is that we have begun to understand it better."[16] Pope John XXIII reigned for five years, the shortest pontificate for two centuries; yet, he transformed the Catholic Church through his inauguration of the Second Vatican Council and set the Church on a new pastoral course. When he died on June 3, 1963, there was considerable sorrow throughout the world and Saint Peter's Square was filled with mourners. It was said that this pope touched the hearts of the human community. Pope John XXIII was buried in the crypt of Saint Peter's Basilica. On December 3, 1963, President Lyndon B. Johnson posthumously awarded him the Presidential Medal of Freedom, the United States' highest civilian award, in recognition of the good relationship between Pope John XXIII and the United States.

Pope Paul VI (1897–1978), Served as Pope during 1963–1978

The Second Vatican Council, begun by Pope John XXIII, was continued by Pope Paul VI. One of the most important marks of this pope related to his insights and determination in shaping the Council and forcing through its reforms. Serving for many years at the Vatican's Secretariat of State, an office headed by a cardinal who acts like a chief of staff to the pope, Pope Paul VI knew about the inner workings of the Vatican and the appropriate means to achieve success. Another mark of this papacy was his encyclical condemning contraception.

Born Giovanni Battista Montini, he was the son of a lawyer and politician. He was ordained in 1920 and served in the office of the Secretariat of State from 1922 through 1954. While serving there, he was also a chaplain of the Catholic student movement from 1924 to 1933. In 1937, he was named as the assistant to the secretary of state to Cardinal Pacelli, who was later Pope Pius XII. In 1944, he was appointed in charge of internal Church affairs and was then largely responsible for organizing the Holy Year of 1950. In November 1954, Monsignor Montini was appointed archbishop of Milan and called himself the "worker's archbishop." His work in Milan included addressing the city's pastoral, social, and industrial problems. He was named cardinal by Pope John XXIII in December 1958. As Cardinal Montini, he made his second visit to the United States in 1960, where he received an honorary degree from the University of Notre Dame.

When Pope John XXIII died in June 1963, the conclave to elect his successor was one of the largest in history, with 81 cardinals eligible to vote. The conclave was deeply divided. Some wanted a change from what was considered a very progressive approach of the Council, while others wanted to see Pope John XXIII's Council policies carried through. Cardinal Montini was in the latter group. After much deliberation and discussion, with all views considered, and after six ballots, Montini, at the age of 65, was elected pope. The newly elected pope took the name Paul VI. When he was crowned pope, he delivered his first address in nine languages. His first order of business was to announce that he intended to continue the work of his predecessor on the Second Vatican Council, and that he would work for the promotion of peace and justice and for the unity of the Christian family of churches.

While this pope was not considered to be radical, despite his determination to continue the work of the Council, he was able to effectively hold the confidence of all but the most diehard. He was able to steer the Council to a successful completion of its work, overseeing the implementation of its reforms while holding together both conservatives and reformers. One of the changes he pushed through was the reform of the Mass and its translation into everyday language, so as to include ordinary people in worship. He also instituted the Synod of Bishops, introduced a compulsory retirement age of 75 for bishops, and decreed that cardinals beyond the age of 80 could not hold office in the Curia, the administrative body of the Vatican, or take part in papal elections. In his efforts to implement the policies of the Council, he also established groups in charge of carrying out the work of the Council.

Pope Paul VI was deeply committed to establishing unity. He traveled to Jerusalem to meet with the leader of the Greek Orthodox Church in 1964, and in 1966, he welcomed the Archbishop of Canterbury on his formal visit to Rome. This was a traveling pope, something new for the papacy. He addressed the United Nations in 1963 and made a speech where he stated "no more war, war never again," which established his role as a moral leader. In 1964, he visited Bombay, India, for the International Eucharistic Congress. In 1969, he visited Geneva for the World Council of Churches. In 1969, he became the first pope to visit Africa, where he ordained bishops, and in 1970, he visited the Philippines and Australia.

Along with his determination that the Second Vatican Council be adopted, something that greatly marked his papacy, Paul VI also had a second issue that greatly marked his reign—that of his strict stand on contraception. While his encyclicals were few, he had several that were considered controversial. In 1967, he published "On the progress of peoples," which "deplored the gap between the rich and the poor nations and which reminded readers that the goods of the earth are intended by God for everyone." That same year, he issued "Priestly celibacy," which "reaffirmed the tradition of obligatory celibacy for Roman Catholic priests." In July 1967, he issued the most controversial, "Of human life," which "declared that every act of sexual intercourse within marriage must be open to the transmission of life, or that there can be no artificial means of contraception." This single encyclical created a great protest throughout the world, and especially in North America and Europe. Pope Paul VI was so shaken by the widespread protests that he vowed to never again publish an encyclical.[17] Pope Paul VI died of a heart attack at Castel Gandolfo, the papal summer home, on August 6, 1978, and was buried in the crypt of Saint Peter's Basilica.

Pope John Paul I (1912–1978), Served as Pope from August 26 to September 28, 1978

Upon the death of Paul VI, another peasant pope was elected, Albino Luciani, the son of a migrant worker. Luciani was a simple, good-humored pastoral bishop who was the first pope to take a dual name. While his tenure as pope lasted only 33 days, his papacy was not the shortest in history. There were 10 popes who served for a few days; the shortest tenure was Pope Urban VII—a pope for only 12 days.

Luciani was ordained in 1935 and served as the curate, a clergy who assisted the rector, at his home parish in a village near Belluno, Italy. By 1937, he was the vice rector and was also a member of the teaching faculty of his seminary. In 1958, he was appointed bishop and was ordained by Pope John XXIII at Saint Peter's Basilica. In 1969, he was named Patriarch of Venice. He attended the Second Vatican Council, and in 1973, he was named cardinal, with the title of San Marco. Luciani was considered to be conservative in his theology and firmly defended Pope Paul VI's encyclical on birth control.

Upon the death of Pope Paul VI in August 1978, in a conclave of cardinals that would be the largest in history, and in a conclave that would begin and end on the same day, Cardinal Luciani was elected on the fourth ballot. Choosing the name John Paul I, in honor of Pope John XXIII and Paul VI, he pledged to continue the implementation of the Second Vatican Council and to promote dialogue with all people, and to promote peace. On September 28, John Paul I was found dead after a heart attack in his Vatican apartment. He had been reading and his reading lamp was still lit when his body was discovered early the next morning. There were rumors surrounding his death, with some charging that he had been poisoned to prevent him from exposing financial corruption within the Vatican Bank. While the rumors were found to be groundless, it was most likely true that he had died from health problems that had been neglected. Pope John Paul I was buried in the crypt of Saint Peter's Basilica.

Pope John Paul II (1920–2005), Served as Pope during 1978–2005

Pope John Paul II was born on May 18, 1920, in Wadowice, Poland, an industrial town southwest of Krakow. He was the first Slav pope and the first non-Italian since Hadrian VI, who reigned during 1522–1523. Known as Karol Wojtyla, he was an outstanding pupil and a fine sportsman; he also loved poetry, and was a particularly good actor. When he was 18, he entered the Jagiellonian University to study Polish language and literature. In 1938, when the Germans occupied Poland, the university was shut down. During the Occupation, he worked as a laborer and a factory worker. In 1942, after the death of his father, Karol heeded the call to priesthood, and because of the Occupation, he secretly began his studies. When Poland was liberated by the Russian Army in January 1945, Karol was able to attend the university once again and graduated with a distinction in theology in August 1946. He was then ordained as a priest in November. In June 1948, he completed his doctorate, and served as a parish priest in Krakow from 1948 through 1951. He then returned to the university to study philosophy, and from 1952 to 1958, he lectured on social ethics at Krakow seminary. In 1956, he was appointed professor of ethics at Lublin, Poland, and was considered one of the country's foremost ethical thinkers. In July 1958, he was elevated to the rank of bishop, and in December 1963, he was named Aarchbishop of Krakow, a role in which he was considered to be politically astute and a vocal adversary to the repressive communist government. In June 1967, he was named cardinal, and during the Second Vatican Council from 1962 to 1965, he became internationally known as a result of his influential contributions to the debate on religious freedom, stating that the Church must grant to others the liberty of thought, action, and speech that the Church itself claimed to possess. By the 1960s and through the 1970s, as cardinal, he became internationally known, traveling to North America, the Middle East, Africa, Asia, and Australia. As pope, he continued to travel and was the most traveled pope in history.

When the cardinals quickly began the consideration of who would be elected as the next pope upon the sudden death of John Paul I, many were looking to elect a younger pope—one with more vitality, and one who could withstand the physical and mental rigors of the office. Many also thought it was time for the pope to be non-Italian. For reasons that included him being so well known and respected throughout the world, Cardinal Wojtyla, the Archbishop of Krakow, was considered. The American and the German cardinals were supportive; they liked his intelligence and charm, and also they noted Karol's particular political pragmatism. On the eighth ballot, Cardinal Wojtyla of Poland was elected pope at the relatively youthful age of 58. He took the name John Paul II because of his "reverence, love, and devotion to John Paul (I) and also to Paul VI, who has been my inspiration, my strength."[18]

When Pope John Paul II addressed the cardinals as the new pope, he stated that he pledged himself to promote the teachings of the Second Vatican Council, and on October 18, he stated that he believed his role to be the witness of a universal love. In March 1979, in his first encyclical, Pope John set out his consistent teaching on human dignity and social justice. His second encyclical in December 1980 was a call for mercy to one another in an increasingly threatened world. On March 13, 1981, as he was being driven through Saint Peter's Square in Rome, Pope John Paul II was shot and seriously wounded by a young man from Turkey. He underwent surgery and convalesced until October 1981. Throughout his years as pope, he called for the rights of workers and the dignity of labor; he argued that freedom of conscience is not absolute since there are issues that are inherently evil; he also declared that women are incapable of receiving holy orders and banned all discussion of the subject.[19]

John Paul II, Pope during 1978–2005, waves to a U.S. audience in 1979. (Library of Congress)

Pope John Paul II placed an emphasis on the global mission of his papacy. He was able to excite his followers with his popular messages on trips throughout the world. His first visit was in January 1979 to Mexico, and in June of that year, he returned to his native Poland. Other countries he visited included Turkey, Great Britain, Fatima, Portugal, and the Netherlands. From 1979 through 2004, Pope John Paul II made over 100 trips, traveling over one million kilometers in all the five continents. His last trip was to Lourdes, France. Every year of his papacy was highlighted by trips even though these journeys proved to be stressful to the resources of the Vatican.

Pope John Paul II was the first pope to write not as "we," but in his own person, as Karol Wojtyla. He believed in religious liberty, and played a key role in emphasizing that topic during the Second Vatican Council. During his youth, after a long friendship with a Jewish boy, he had always nurtured a keen interest in Judaism, and he was the first pope to visit the Roman Synagogue; he also established diplomatic relations with the state of Israel. He also had openness towards other religions and initiated worship with Muslims, Hindus, the Buddhists, and Shamans. He was a former university professor of philosophy and a published poet and playwright. He was a practiced mountaineer and skier, a skilled linguist in French, German, English, Italian, and Russian, besides Polish. He saw himself as a universal bishop, meaning he felt it important for pastoral visits to every corner of the world, carrying his message of old-fashioned moral values and faithfulness to the teachings of the Church, using his energy and charisma that brought the faithful out in millions, likened to fans at a football match or extreme supporters at a rally.

There is no doubt that John Paul II was one of the most popular leaders of the Catholic Church. From the early 1990s, Pope John Paul II suffered from various health issues, which were never discussed outside of the Vatican until 2003, when it was clear he was suffering from Parkinson's disease. Upon his death in 2005, more than four million people came to the Vatican for the funeral service, attended by government officials, presidents, prime ministers, and members of other churches.

From a friendship that began during the Second Vatican Council, Pope John Paul II called on his good friend to serve in an important capacity and to be close by in the Vatican. In 1981, Pope John Paul II called Bishop Joseph Ratzinger to Rome as Prefect of the Congregation for the Doctrine of the Faith. In 1993, he elevated Bishop Ratzinger to the rank of cardinal bishop, and in 2002, named him dean of the College of Cardinals. In this capacity, Cardinal Bishop Ratzinger presided at and preached the homily at the funeral mass for John Paul II.

A conclave to elect a new pope quickly convened and the secret vote was nearly just as swift. Cardinal Ratzinger, the good friend and the cardinal who presided for more than 20 years as the "watch-dog" of the Church as the Prefect of the Doctrine of Faith, was elevated to pope; the cardinal who worked with John Paul II for almost a quarter of a century and who spoke so eloquently at the funeral mass rose from the others to be considered the next pope. Benedict XVI's life was easily and naturally given to the Church when he was a young boy in Bavaria, and while he stated he never wanted to be pope, he said it was God's will for him to wear the shoes of the fisherman and sit on the throne to direct the Church and to be one of the most powerful leaders in the world. Now, since 2005, Benedict XVI has been the pope. The whole of his life has been given to the Catholic Church; since he was a child, he has been influenced by the history of the Church and by all the popes who came before him, especially the modern popes of the 20th century. This biography will provide an insight into the influences, beliefs, and motivations of the man who is the leader of the Catholic Church.

NOTES

1. Cindy Wooden, "Statistically Speaking: Vatican Numbers Hint at Fading Faith Practice," *National Catholic Reporter*, August 17, 2012, http://ncronline.org.

2. Bart McDowell, *Inside the Vatican* (Washington, DC: National Geographic Society, 1991), 16.

3. Vatican: The Holy See, http://www.vaticanstate.va.

4. Richard P. McBrien, *Lives of the Popes* (San Francisco: Harper-SanFrancisco, 1997), 403–410.

5. Ibid., 417.

6. Eamon Duffy, *Saints & Sinners: A History of the Popes* (New Haven, CT: Yale University Press, 1997), 245.

7. McBrien, *Lives of the Popes*, 488.

8. Ibid., 359.

9. Ibid., 360.

10. Ibid., 362.

11. Duffy, *Saints & Sinners: A History of the Popes*, 262.

12. Ibid., 263.

13. Ibid., 264.

14. McBrien, *Lives of the Popes*, 371.

15. Ibid., 440.

16. Ibid., 374.

17. Ibid., 380.

18. Ibid., 387.

19. J.N.D. Kelly and M.J. Walsh, *Oxford Dictionary of Popes* (Oxford: Oxford University Press, 1986), 333.

Chapter 2

THE EARLY YEARS

"From our parents we learned what it means to have hold in the faith in God. . . . When the religious life is already practiced in the family, it influences the whole rest of your life. This forms your whole life and directs it towards God. It creates a fertile ground for the priestly vocation."

—*Monsignor Georg Ratzinger*[1]

To narrate the story of Pope Benedict XVI, it is important to begin where his story began—the formative years that profoundly shaped him. This man was, and is, in many ways, like many of the men elected pope before him. Like other popes, he possesses a profound, unwavering faith, and like others throughout history, this pope too came from humble beginnings. However, the years of Benedict XVI's youth were as difficult and as different from those of other popes who came before him. Perhaps, even the circumstance of his very birth was a sign of what he would become.

Joseph Aloysius Ratzinger was born to parents Joseph and Maria on April 16, 1927, in the Bavarian town of Marktl am Inn, Germany. It was the eve of Easter, Holy Saturday, a snowy, frigid day, not unusual in the town unofficially known as the "Little market on the river Inn" located on the Austrian border. Joseph's father was a rural police officer and supervisor. His mother was a skilled cook who usually worked in the small hotels in the area—what today would be called bed and breakfast inns. His parents were married in 1920. His father died in 1959 at the age of 82 and his mother died in 1963, at the age of 79. Joseph later described his father as giving him a "critical mind," and his mother instilling in him a "warm hearted religious sense." Joseph said his father went to church three times on Sundays—at 6:00 a.m., at 9:00 a.m. for the main liturgy, and again for the afternoon devotional services.[2] Joseph had an older sister, Maria, born in 1921, and an older brother, Georg, born in 1924, named after his great uncle. It was Maria who financially supported the family while both Joseph and his brother attended seminary. Georg also became a priest and was later a monsignor, and the director of a well-known choir that toured the world and also performed at the Vatican. Maria was Joseph's secretary and housekeeper later in life and always had a particular influence on her brother and his decisions.

While Joseph's birth was certainly heralded by his parents and family, the circumstances were somewhat auspicious, especially in light of what infant Joseph would become. The water used for Joseph's baptism had been newly blessed for Easter, perhaps a symbol of Joseph's future life. He later wrote, "To be the first person baptized with the new water was seen as a significant act of Providence. I have always been filled with thanksgiving for having had my life immersed in this way in the Easter mystery, since this could only be a sign of blessing . . . the more I reflect on it, the more this seems to be fitting for the nature of our human life: we are still awaiting Easter; we are not yet standing in the full light but walking toward it full of trust."[3]

THE GLOW OF THE ALPS
AND THE GLOOM OF NAZISM

Joseph's childhood was spent within a triangle of land about 40 miles across and 40 miles long that is bordered on the west by the River Inn, on the east by the River Salzach, and on the south by the Alps; despite its area of about 160 miles, there is no urban center. Rather, it consists of a number of small villages and hamlets. For Joseph, it was the lush forests and mountains that he remembered throughout his life and they became a place he wanted to return to when he retired. He often said he could smell the flowers and the freshness of the trees; he could still see how the homes were decorated, and could hear the music and the voices taking part in the religious festivals. Dating back to the 16th century, when Bavaria became a strictly Catholic state, it was Bavarian Catholicism, with its liturgy, rituals, and processions that were profoundly steeped in his youth, and what he would always remember. It was all of these circumstances, along with his family, that formed who he was, who he became, and what his religious life would require. The people of his life, along with his family, were the people of the Church; the beautiful setting and how his family and neighbors lived in their rituals of faith also had a profound effect on him. It was surely because of his early years spent in the small villages and hamlets of Bavaria that were so idyllic, and remembered so vividly throughout his life, that the outside world at the time was seemingly so frightful.

When Joseph was born in 1927, Germany was still reeling from the effects of World War I. Because of the circumstances of how the war began and how it finally ended four years later, and how Germany was blamed for the war itself, Germany was forced to pay war reparations set at the Treaty of Versailles ratified on June 28, 1919, by the Allies, Britain, France, and America. The settlement agreed to at Versailles, France, crippled Germany as it tried to move towards a democracy following its defeat in the war. As a boy in Bavaria, Germany, young Joseph and his family moved four times before he was 10 years old. Despite these upheavals during his early life, he always remembered each town in Bavaria affectionately, and as a child, he was only somewhat aware of the continued economic devastation that permeated the country. The high unemployment rate and soaring food prices, along with a currency that became worthless, all made life more than difficult for most inhabitants. Yet, young Joseph's life in Bavaria was tranquil, and his life was sheltered from such difficulties. Since his father was a police officer, he provided his family with a steady income, unlike the area's farmers who were solely dependent on their crops.

Joseph's parents were deeply religious and the home was filled with symbols of their faith. The singing of hymns and reading and reciting devotions were a part of everyday life. Joseph developed a love of read-ing and many of his days were spent outside, where he was absorbed in literature. Along with reading, Joseph's love of music grew out of the rich musical culture of Bavaria and from his family's love of singing. Joseph played the piano, and his love of Beethoven and Mozart developed at an early age. His love of Mozart's music, in particular, stayed with him into adulthood. He once noted, "It is so luminous and yet at the same time so deep. It contains the whole tragedy of human existence."[4] If Joseph was absorbed in music and literature, he was neither interested in, nor particularly good at sports. He enjoyed hiking and playing with his friends, and was naturally nurtured by the landscape and by his close-knit family. Writing about hiking with his mother and siblings, he noted that they would often go on hikes to a chapel in a place where they absorbed the peace, and that the place of his childhood was the "land of dreams."[5] It was religious faith, family, and the climate and culture of where he grew up that were his greatest early influences. The Church and its liturgies and rites left lasting impressions on Joseph and formed his views right into priesthood and on to the Vatican.

Toward the end of 1932, Joseph's father decided to move the family to a new home in Ashau am Inn. The change was the result of the Nazi movement and activities of the brownshirts, and his father's outspo-kenness against their activities in their former home in Tittmoning, the second home since young Joseph's birth in 1927. While Joseph had little memory of his birthplace in Marktl—since his family left there in 1929, barely two years after his birth—it is Tittmoning that Pope Bene-dict XVI says is his childhood's land of dreams. The town square with its splendid fountain, the Salzburg-style architecture, and the shop win-dows illuminated at Christmas time were particularly special memories. Still, the town and the surrounding area experienced difficult economic times and an intensifying and complex political climate. More often, his father found himself taking a position against the violence of the Nazis at public meetings, and the worries of what might happen in the future were difficult for him to bear. The move to another town shortly before Christmas of 1932 was a satisfying one in that the family moved into pleasant quarters in a modern country house leased to the rural police. The offices were on the ground floor and the Ratzinger family lived on the second floor. On the village square were the church, the school, and a restaurant. In the middle of the village was a brewery and restaurant that was the men's meeting place on Sundays. The village church was less grand than the church in Tittmoning, and the stores were plainer, which at first was somewhat of a letdown for Joseph and his siblings; however, soon all of the family grew fond of the village and appreciated its own kind of Bavarian beauty.

At just five years of age, Joseph happened to be in the village square when a black limousine carrying the archbishop of Munich came into town. As he stepped out of the large automobile, he was greeted by children, including young Joseph, who was smitten by what he saw. Later, he told his father that he wanted to grow up to be a cardinal. It was not because of the large black auto that swept into the village and excited all the children. Instead, it was the cardinal himself, commanding in his presence and dressed in his black robe. It was this dream, which originated that day, that never left Joseph.

There was another event—certainly not as positive as the large black automobile and the arrival of the archbishop in the village square—that was happening in 1932. This was the year that Adolf Hitler's National Socialist Party became the largest political party in the legislative assembly of the government of Germany. In late January 1933, Adolf Hitler was named chancellor of the Reich. In later years, many thought that all Germans were part of the Nazi party, Hitler's own political party, and that German Catholics also belonged to this party. However, when Joseph was just a boy, his father, Joseph Ratzinger Senior, a policeman, and by then a minor government official, had much to say about the Reich and Hitler, and likely should have kept silent while attending town government meetings; however, he typically did not. His courage in speaking against Nazi officials was founded in his strong Catholic faith. Joseph's brother Georg remembered it this way, "Our father was a bitter enemy of Nazism because he believed it was in conflict with our faith. That was the example he set for us." And a younger Joseph Ratzinger said that his father was a man with " 'unfailing clairvoyance' who saw that Hitler's victory would not be a victory for Germany, but would instead be a victory for the Antichrist that would bring a disastrous future for all believers."[6]

At this time, as Nazism was widespread throughout the country, it was clear that nationalist socialism was transforming life throughout the cities and villages of Germany, including Joseph's own Bavaria. All throughout Germany at the time, and even for those who felt as the elder Ratzinger did, everyone was required to take part in everything dictated by the Nazi party and all were required to, outwardly at least, believe in all that the Nazi government espoused. For instance, when Hitler was named Chancellor, everyone was required to celebrate; children took part in parades held throughout Germany, including the village where the Ratzinger family lived. Those that supported a new Nazi government, who had before kept silent and lived in secret, could now live in the open; as a result of their party-supported allegiance, they deliberately inflicted terror among other residents. In December 1936, the Hitler Youth Law was passed. This law said that it was the duty of all 14-year-olds to enter the Hitler Youth or League of German Girls programs. It stated that all Aryan youth, white people of non-Semitic descent, were required to attend party meetings, take part in outings, and support and promote the party's teachings. This allegiance applied to the Ratzinger family too, including Georg, Joseph, and Maria, much to the dismay of their father. Further, everyone who worshiped at the Catholic Church was required to inform on priests who were believed to be enemies of the Reich. Later, Joseph proudly said that his father did not and would not have had any part in this and instead warned priests if he knew they were in danger.

In the midst of what was happening throughout Germany, life continued on. When Joseph was 10 years old, he and his family moved outside the city of Traunstein. Because of the physical demands and constant stresses of serving in the police force, policemen were required to retire at the age of 60. Joseph's father eagerly waited for the day he could leave his job. While the night shifts proved to be difficult for his father, it was the increasing stress and political party expectations that gave his father the most problems. In early March 1937, Joseph Senior turned 60 and the family moved to a farmhouse they had purchased in 1933, just outside of Traunstein. On one side of the property were oak trees and on the other, a pine forest, and while there was no running water inside the house, there was an abundance of fresh water from a well. The family home became a paradise for the three Ratzinger children. From the gardens to the meadow, to the forest and grove of trees—and in the boys' upstairs bedroom where they felt they could almost touch the mountains

from their window—it was an idyllic place to live during a very tumultu-
ous political time and was a place that Joseph has always remembered.

In Traunstein, Joseph's brother became an altar boy and entered the
gymnasium, a secondary school where the emphasis was on academic
subjects rather than technical training. He later entered the seminary.
Joseph's sister, Maria, attended a middle school for girls in a nearby convent run by Franciscan sisters. Joseph entered a "humanistic" *gymnasium*,
a school for the study of classical languages. Here, he was the youngest
and the smallest of the students in the class. Joseph proved to be a brilliant
student, especially in the study of Greek and Latin. Later, when Latin
was removed as the official language of the Catholic mass at the
Second Vatican Council of 1962, Joseph continued to believe that at
least some of the mass should be in Latin.

After several years of study, Joseph was advised by his pastor to attend Saint Michael's Seminary, a school similar to a religious high
school that assimilated youth towards a religious calling; this school was
also referred to as a minor seminary. This was the first step of Joseph's
ecclesiastical calling. On his father's limited retirement income, it was
difficult to pay for such schooling. Fortunately, Maria had received her
diploma and found a job, which helped the family's budget. During Easter 1939, Joseph became a student at the seminary. Because his older
brother, Georg, had earlier entered the same seminary, Joseph already
knew some of his classmates and he easily made friends of his own. However, this was a boarding school and staying there instead of at home
proved difficult for young Joseph. Suddenly, he was immersed into the
strict discipline and the rigid schedule that incorporated exercise and
study. Students woke at 5:00 a.m. and attended mass at 6:30 a.m.; then,
they attended classes after breakfast until early afternoon, followed by
study that lasted well into the evening. The students regularly participated in exercise that included rugby and football, which was distress-
ing to young Joseph, who was younger, smaller, and notably physically
weaker than his classmates; he was also insecure in his athletic abili-
ties and was markedly behind his peers in playing sports. The other
boys quickly recognized their classmate's intellectual mind and that his
prowess was not on the playing field; to assist him in the required exercise, the boys taught him how to play and also how to be a teammate,
rather than be solitary and totally absorbed in his studies.

Joseph later wrote that he had to learn how to fit into the group and build a community with others, both in giving and receiving. He noted that his experiences at Saint Michael's and his friendships built there were very important in his later life.[7] Joseph was quickly gauged as an avid, remarkably intelligent student, and a young man who loved books and music, and above all, the music of Mozart. He was also enthralled with the Church and with all things related to religion. The church year gave him a rhythm to live by—Advent, Lent, Easter, and the Eucharistic liturgy, along with the German missal, or prayer book, all made deep impressions on him and gave shape and meaning to the young man's life, which continued throughout the years.

A CONSCRIPT IN THE GERMAN ARMY

By the time Joseph was in his early teens, Nazi troops had entered Denmark, Norway, Holland, Belgium, Luxembourg, and France. The Balkans were next for Hitler's domination, and in 1941, as Hitler launched his attack on the Soviet Union, Joseph was well aware that his life would soon change dramatically. Now, for the people of his beloved Bavaria and all of Germany, war was the great reality. German troops entered his village, and many of the homes were taken as headquarters, including the Ratzinger home. The seminary was needed as a military hospital, and all seminarians were sent home, including Joseph and his brother. All convent schools had been closed by the Nazis, so seminary students moved there for classes. Despite a war that seemed to be still far away, yet certainly threatening with every bit of news of Nazi advancements, Joseph built a community with others and later noted that he was very grateful for a time that was very important in his life.[8]

In the summer of 1942, Georg was drafted into the *Reichsarbeitsdienst*, the work service of the Reich. In the fall, he was drafted into the army and was made a radio operator in the signal corps. By 1944, his tour of duty included France, Holland, Czechoslovakia, and the Italian front. There, he was wounded and he returned to convalesce at the same seminary where he and his brother had studied. Once his wounds healed, he was sent back to Italy. During this time, Joseph continued his studies in classical languages and mathematics and also developed an even greater love of literature. Despite progressing in his studies, he was well aware of the continued toll of the war, including the deaths of many of his classmates.

By this time, the Germans had suffered devastating losses. Many of their troops had been killed or were wounded. The Reich developed a new way of reinforcing their troops. They determined that all youth, born in 1926 and 1927, and attending boarding schools and seminaries, should be drafted into the antiaircraft defense, Flugabwehr, known as Flak, which would allow them to continue their studies while being trained to defend against enemy aircraft. Even though Joseph was living at home at the time while continuing his religious studies, he was still considered a student at the seminary and was determined eligible to be a draftee. In 1943, when Joseph was just 16, he became a conscript of the German Army.

His first post was at the antiaircraft unit stationed at Obergrashof, near Munich, where he was trained to spot enemy planes. Writing while he was a cardinal, in his book *Milestones, Memoirs 1927–1977*, he notes that at 16 years of age, he had to undertake a "very peculiar kind of 'boarding-school' existence." He and his fellow seminarians had to live in barracks like regular soldiers, wore uniforms similar to regular soldiers, and yet unlike regular soldiers, carried a reduced load of studies, given by the teachers of the famous Maximilians Gymnasium.[9]

At Obergrashof, one of Joseph's fellow conscripts remembered him as a "very reserved, fairly inconspicuous figure." While inspecting the unit where the boys were lined up at attention, a high-ranking officer, who was likely to be very intimidating, asked each of them what they wanted to be as an adult. Several said they wanted to be a pilot, others said tank commanders or engineers, but when the officer came to Joseph, his unexpected response was that he wanted to be a parish priest. While some of the boys laughed, one remembered that "to give such an answer took courage." Confronting a representative of a totalitarian power, and also his fellow teenagers, took more than just courage; it also took confidence created by a deep faith.[10]

Joseph's military career was unusual in that while he trained and while his unit was assigned to guard a branch of the Bavarian Motor Works (BMW), his weapon, and that of his fellow soldiers, was not loaded. While in uniform, his military duties were light; however, he did witness war's atrocities. At the BMW plant, he saw laborers sent from a branch of the infamous Dachau concentration camp; he also saw Hungarian Jews shipped out of sight, to their deaths elsewhere. His time in the military did leave him time to study and time for spiritual growth. Towards the end of his military service, his unit was sent to Gilching, a town southwest of Munich. There was also time for organized Catholic religious studies and worship. At Gilching, Joseph and the other soldiers had a double commission—defending the Dornier-Werke, a German aircraft manufacturer, and to stop the Allied forces from an attack on Munich. Despite being in military service, Cardinal Ratzinger later wrote that he remembered his time in Gilching fondly. The officer who was in charge of the soldiers there defended their autonomy, including keeping them from having to participate in military exercises, and enabling young Joseph to have private quarters. In addition, there was a large group of Catholics stationed there who organized religious instruction and visits to local churches. While this part of his service is remembered as pleasant, it was also quite difficult. Early in 1943, his group was attacked by the Allies, leaving one of his fellow soldiers dead and many wounded. In the summer of that year, the attacks on Munich began, and when he was allowed to travel into the city to attend classes, he was more frightened to see the devastation, with the city falling into ruin. When the Allied forces began the invasion of France, Ratzinger wrote in his book *Milestones*, many looked on this as a sign of hope. He wrote, "There was a great trust in the Western powers," and that "their sense of justice would also help Germany to begin a new and peaceful existence."[11]

In September 1944, Joseph was released from the antiaircraft unit, and by the time he returned home, his draft notice for regular military service had arrived. Just 10 days later, he joined his unit in a camp located where the borders of Austria, Czechoslovakia, and Hungary meet, about 200 miles from his home. Members of a group of Nazi partisans called the Austrian Legion were in charge of his unit; this group had originally formed in the early 1930s. Cardinal Ratzinger later wrote that his time in the labor detail left him with oppressive memories and that the leaders of the group were "fanatical ideologues who tyrannized them without respite."[12]

Because he admitted that he intended to become a Catholic priest, he was able to escape the worst of the constant abuse, but was, however, the butt of countless, continuous religious insults. For some time,

Joseph was kept in a labor detail; yet, he was never sent to the line of battle, which was drawing ever closer. In November 1944, Joseph was given civilian clothes and was put on a train for home. While at home, he anticipated he would receive yet another call to serve in a forward battle unit, and a short time later, he was ordered to Munich, where he joined a unit under the command of an officer who hated the war, hated the Nazis, and cared for his troops. Joseph spent the Christmas of 1944 in a barracks with other dispirited men, all tired of the long and devastating war. In January 1945, Joseph's unit was moved about, and with Hitler's death, Joseph decided in the spring to leave his unit and return home. Taking the back roads, hoping to avoid the soldiers who were ordered to shoot deserters, Joseph came upon two soldiers at a railroad underpass. As the situation grew tense, they noticed that Joseph had his arm in a sling from a slight wound, and the two war-weary soldiers told Joseph to move on, believing that, like them, he too had enough of war, and the injury was enough of an excuse to let him go.

When Joseph arrived home, he found that his family home had been turned into a boarding house. Living there were two English nuns, a sergeant major of the air force, a Catholic from Berlin, and in time, two SS men who were also given shelter. Joseph worried that he might be deemed a deserter by the SS men, as it was obvious that he was of military age; however, both were gone within a day and any danger was averted. The Americans arrived in Joseph's village in the spring of 1945, and chose the Ratzinger house as the headquarters. Because Joseph had served in the German Army, he was sent to a prisoner of war camp. Before leaving, he was able to fill his pockets with pencils and a notebook, allowing him to write and sketch during his imprisonment. In June 1945, Joseph was released and he hitchhiked home. In July, his brother Georg found his way home from Italy, and together, they helped restore the buildings at Saint Michael's seminary, which had been used as a hospital for wounded German soldiers. Instead of students at the minor seminary, they were an enthusiastic building repair crew, working again for a cause they deeply believed in. In the autumn, the brothers moved to Freising to enter the major seminary.

The war years were pivotal for Joseph, teaching him important lessons that he would later bring to his life as a priest, theologian, cardinal, and pope. One lesson he learned was the measure of human lives. Joseph had

a cousin who was about his own age, and who was mentally handi-
capped. When they were both 14, the Nazis took his cousin away for
what they said "was therapy, but was in fact, euthanasia."[13] What Joseph
learned after the war surpassed even the darkest of fears. There were the
concentration camps and the genocide of the Jews, and specifically, the
Dachau concentration camp located near Munich. Joseph's brother,
Georg, wrote in his book *My Brother, the Pope* that anti-Semitism was
never an issue in their family or within their sphere of acquaintances.
He wrote that the Ratzinger family considered everyone as a fellow
human being, even if he was a Nazi, although they were cautious
about the Nazis from the beginning and kept their distance. They were
not, he wrote, acquainted with any Jews, and did not hear about the
anti-Semitic outrages of 1933, the *Kristallnacht*, the "Night of Broken
Glass," which happened on the night of November 9, 1938—a night
when the Nazis and their sympathizers in Germany and Austria engaged
in attacks on Jews and their property, or of the deportation of Jews. In
school, Georg wrote, in the Saturday course titled "National Socialist
Ideology," they were taught that Jews were wicked.[14]

THE ISSUES OF THE CHURCH, THE POPES, AND THE JEWS

Pope Pius XII was elected pope in 1939, at the beginning of declarations
of war in Europe, and prior to the United States entering the war. Pius
XII had a history with Germany, having served as nuncio in Germany
for many years, a post appointment by Pope Pius XI. He was fluent in
German and had great affection for the German people and their culture.
When he was elected pope, he condemned Nazi policies and their inherent racism. He was deeply committed to his role as the spiritual leader of
all nations and for world peace, and struggled with the expectation of taking sides and tried to promote peace and prevent atrocities. Despite all
his continued efforts, over time, he became indecisive in his decisions and
about what he and the Vatican could do against Hitler and the Nazis. The
official Church's teachings clearly were against the Nazis' racial policies;
however, as the war continued, Pius XII was under pressure to speak out
against the genocide and Nazi atrocities. As pressure by the Italian Jewish
community mounted, he opened religious houses as places of refuge.

As pope during World War II, Pius XII was called "Hitler's Pope." Catholics were accused of everything, from cheering on the persecution of the Jews to encouraging Hitler's anti-Semitism from their pulpits. The next pope also had a history with the Nazis and the Catholic Church's dealings with the Jewish people. After Pius XII died in 1958, Pope John XXIII was elected as pope. During the war and the German occupation of Greece, as Father Roncalli, he tried to do what he could to relieve the distress of the Greek people and also tried to prevent the deportation of Jews. In 1944, he was appointed as nuncio to France, where he dealt with the reputation of bishops thought to have collaborated with the pro-Nazi Vichy regime.

The next reigning pope with a connection to the Nazi regime was Pope John Paul II, who lived and studied in Poland during the German Occupation that began in 1938. At the time, John Paul II was studying language and literature at university. When the school was shut down by the Germans, John Paul II, known as Karol Wojtyla at the time, was forced by the occupying regime to work as a laborer, and later a factory worker. In 1942, he felt a call to the priesthood; however, he had to study secretly. Upon the liberation of Poland by the Russian Army in 1945, Karol returned to school, and in time, obtained his doctorate and served as a parish priest in Krakow, Poland. During his boyhood, he had a long friendship with a Jewish boy, and throughout his life, had a keen interest in Judaism. As pope, John Paul II was the first pope to visit a Jewish synagogue, and he also established diplomatic relations with the state of Israel.

> That the Jews are connected with God in a special way and that God does not allow that bond to fail is entirely obvious. We wait for the instant in which Israel will say yes to Christ, but we know that it has a special mission in history now . . . which is significant for the world.
>
> —Joseph Cardinal Ratzinger and Peter Seewald,
> *God and the World*[15]

The next reigning pope to answer questions about the relationship between Catholics and Jews was Pope Benedict XVI. Prior to his election as pope, when he served as a parish priest, then as a bishop and on to archbishop, Joseph reacted to what happened in his country during World War II, to his German nationality, to his membership in the Hitler Youth program, and to serving in the German Army at posts near Munich and at the border of Austria and Hungary. In 1977, when he was elevated to the rank of archbishop of Munich and Freising, he had a responsibility, established in 1933 between Hitler and the Vatican, which required Germany's Roman Catholic archbishops to "take an oath of loyalty to the state." This oath required that he raise his hand before the Minister-President of Bavaria and state: "Before God and the Holy Gospel, I swear and promise, as is fitting for a bishop, allegiance to Germany and Bavaria."[16]

When Joseph was the archbishop of Munich, his residence was near the memorial site to the Dachau concentration camp, just one such camp where atrocities against the Jews were carried out by the Nazis. It was also at this camp where more than 2,500 Catholic priests and seminarians were incarcerated, and where they were required to work, subjected to medical experiments and tortured by S.S. guards. When the Dachau camp was liberated in April 1945, nearly half of the more than 2,500 priests were dead.[17] Despite the short distance to the camp from the archbishop's residence in Munich, there is no record of Joseph ever having made a public statement about Dachau during his tenure as archbishop. According to Timothy Ryback, in his article entitled "Forgiveness," which appeared in *The New Yorker* in 2006, in March 1980, Joseph was in Dachau to confirm Roman Catholic youths at the Holy Cross Church, and in August 1980, he returned to Dachau for a profession of two Carmelite sisters. One convent sister, who shared a meal with Joseph, verified that he did not visit the memorial site at the time, as did Sister Irmengard, the prioress at the Holy Blood Convent, which oversees the Dachau memorial. Irmengard also stated that Joseph had visited Auschwitz with Pope John Paul II and that "he had made explicit statements about the Holocaust, and that he had helped pioneer reconciliation between Catholics and Jews." She added that Joseph "had been the archbishop of Munich for less than five years," and "cautioned (Ryback) against reading too much into his apparent avoidance of the former camp."[18] Walter Brugger, a prelate in Freising, noted, "In his years as archbishop . . . his main concern was to grow into his pastoral duties, his bishopric, his parishioners, the clergy, his fellow brothers," and that he had known Joseph for nearly five decades and had observed that Joseph had spent his career as an academic. Winfried Rohmel, the head of the diocese press office, suggested another reason, "In Cardinal Ratzinger's four-year tenure as archbishop, there was no event that would have occasioned his presence at the concentration camp, as was the case with his predecessors."[19]

In *The New Yorker* article of 2006, author Ryback describes Joseph's visit to France to deliver papal blessings at the commemoration of the 60th anniversary of the Allied landings in Normandy in June 1944. As cardinal, Joseph joined more than a dozen government leaders, including the French president Jacques Chirac, the German chancellor Gerhard Schroder, Russian president Vladimir Putin, Queen Elizabeth II, and U.S. president George W. Bush, in several ceremonies, including one on the beach at the French town of Arromanches and another held at the American Cemetery at Omaha Beach. He also visited another cemetery, La Combe, to "pay his respects to the twenty-one thousand German war dead buried there." Also interned there were members of the Waffen S.S. Panzer division, an elite military arm of the Nazis regime. "The dead also included Michael Wittmann, a legendary tank commander, and Adolf Diekmann, a major-Sturmbannfuhrer—who oversaw the massacre of villagers in nearby Ordour-sur-Glane. Of the six hundred and forty-two victims, two hundred and thirty-one were children; only six villagers survived." While visiting the cemetery, Joseph said, "In this hour, we bow in respect to the dead of the Second World War. We remember the many young people from our homeland whose futures and hopes were destroyed in the bloody slaughter of the war. As Germans, we cannot help but be painfully moved to realize that their idealism and their obedience to the state were misused by an unjust government." Joseph "regretted that Pflicht—the blind and unquestioning obedience to duty, a distinctly Germanic quality—had been exploited for evil purposes," but he insisted that this had in no way "dishonored the service and sacrifice rendered to the fatherland." He said, "They simply tried to do their duty—even if beset by terrible inner conflicts, doubts, and questions." On his visit, he did not mention the Waffen S.S. soldiers, but said "that it was not within [his] spiritual commission to judge the fallen of La Cambe, into whose conscience only God can see."[20] During his visit to the small cemetery, which attracted little media attention, Joseph stated that for "the origins of the Second World War, [he] blamed the Allies, particularly the French, for driving the Germans into the twelve-year nightmare of Nazi rule," adding, "Animosity and bitterness remained between the combatant nations after the First World War, especially between the Germans and the French, resulting in a poisoning of the nations' souls." He said, "The Treaty of Versailles was deliberately intended to humiliate Germany and to burden the country with so much debt that it radicalized the people . . . opening the door to dictatorship, and to belief in its deceptive promises of the return of freedom, honor, and might to Germany." He added, "The German people had been doubly victimized: humiliated by their French neighbors; seduced and deceived by Nazi leaders. National pride had been wounded; collective humiliation had been exploited. War and destruction were the outcome. 'An eye for an eye, a tooth for a tooth'—that does not lead to peace. We have seen the results. . . . Thank God the same thing was not repeated after the Second World War. The Americans generously helped us Germans with their Marshall Plan, helped us rebuild our country, and made prosperity and freedom possible."[21]

As pope, Benedict XVI has long realized the responsibility and obligation of reconciliation between the Jews and the Catholic Church. He has visited more synagogues than any of his predecessors, including visiting one in Cologne, Germany, in 2005, another in New York in 2008, and yet another in Rome in 2010. In Auschwitz, Germany, at the sight of one of the concentration camps and at the Holocaust Memorial Yad Vashem, he denounced any form of anti-Semitism or anti-Jewish sentiment. In Jerusalem, he prayed at the Wailing Wall. After his installation as pope, he wrote to the Jewish community in Rome and was the first pope to invite a rabbi to address the Synod of Bishops. When he became pope in 2005, many Jewish organizations welcomed his election. Israel Singer, who was president of the World Jewish Congress at the time, stated that "as Prefect of the Congregation for the Doctrine of the Faith, Ratzinger had articulated the basic structure of the foundations between the two world religions." He added that Ratzinger, as prefect, "changed the two-thousand year history of relations between Judaism and Christianity for the better."[22] When asked whether his first official act as pope—to write a letter to the Jewish community of Rome—was a symbolic gesture meant to convey a basic thrust of his pontificate,

Benedict XVI answered that "it clearly was and that as a German, what happened in the Third Reich, which was a special reason to look with humility and shame and with love, upon the People of Israel." He added, "During [his] studies and later as a theologian, things came together and began to shape the course of my thinking as a theologian . . . that this new, loving, sympathetic interrelations of Israel and the Church, where each respects the being and distinctive mission of the other, had to play an essential part in my proclamation of the Christian faith."[23]

In August 2005, as pope, Benedict XVI spoke to Jewish representatives in Cologne in a synagogue destroyed during the 1938 *Kristallnacht* pogrom. In his remarks, he recalled the Nazi persecution of the Jews as "the darkest period of German and European history." He said, "The Catholic Church has a duty to remember the Holocaust and to teach its lessons to younger generations who did not witness the 'terrible events' that took place before and during World War II." He said, "Christians and Jews have to respect each other . . . and love each other."[24]

In 2008, marking the 70th anniversary of *Kristallnacht*—"Night of Broken Glass," Benedict XVI noted that he had been 11 years old on the night of November 9, 1938, the night of the *Kristallnacht*. He said, "I still feel pain for what happened in that tragic circumstance, whose memory must serve to ensure that similar horrors are never repeated again and that we commit ourselves, at every level, to fighting anti-Semitism and discrimination, especially by educating the younger generations in respect and mutual acceptance." Marking the anniversary, Benedict asked Catholics to pray for the Jewish victims of the Holocaust and said he "condemned all forms of anti-Semitism."[25]

Just as their German heritage and their close-knit family were, and are, important to Benedict XVI as pope and throughout his life as a Catholic, young Joseph and his family and friends' lives and beliefs were greatly influenced by the war and by what happened in their country during the Nazi regime and after. It was their unwavering faith, passed on to Joseph and his brother by their mother and father that allowed for them to weather the difficult, austere, and dangerous war years. In his book *My Brother, the Pope*, Monsignor Georg Ratzinger, Benedict XVI's older brother, drew a picture of their family that grew strong through the practice of its deep faith that could withstand the storms of their time in Bavaria, especially of the time of the

Nazi regime. He relates the story of their father, who was very angry and also very worried about Hitler and the Nazis coming to power, and how in their father's view, Hitler was wicked and an evil criminal. The book recounts that throughout Germany, Hitler wanted the Catholic schools to be subordinate to the state alone and teach the ideology of the Führer. It was the politics of the day that influenced Joseph's home, religious, and the educational life. At the time of his first communion in 1934, Joseph's father bought him his own missal translated into German. This became one of the most important guides of Joseph's life.[26]

From his mandatory membership in the Hitler Youth program, which his father vehemently opposed, but which was nonetheless required of all youth, to his religious training at the seminary that was eventually closed by the Nazis, to his conscription into the Army in his teens, to his time in the P.O.W. camp, to continuing his religious studies after the war and entering the priesthood, Joseph's formative years in Bavaria over the two decades of war and deprivation significantly influenced who he became—parish priest, theologian, professor, archbishop, cardinal, and eventually Pope Benedict XVI. In May 2005, just after his election as pope, Benedict XVI met with diplomats accredited to the Vatican. In his address, he emphasized his awareness of contemporary history. He also acknowledged his German heritage and that he had an appreciation for those involved in war, stating that he himself had lived through World War II. He said, "For my part, I come from a country in which peace and fraternity have a great place in the heart of its inhabitants, in particular, of those who, like me, knew war and the separation of brothers belonging to the same nation, because of devastating and inhuman ideologies that, cloaked in dreams and illusion, imposed on human beings the yoke of oppression. You will understand therefore that I am particularly sensitive to dialogue among all people, to overcome all forms of conflict and tension, and to make our world a world of peace and fraternity. Uniting efforts, all together, the Christian communities, leaders of nations, diplomats, and all people of goodwill, are called to realize a peaceful society to overcome the temptation of the clash between cultures, ethnic groups, and different worlds. To achieve this, every nation must draw from its spiritual and cultural heritage the best values of which it is bearer, to go out without fear to meet the other, ready to share its spiritual and material riches for the common good."[27]

NOTES

1. Michael Hesemann, "Brothers in Faith: How the Ratzinger Boys Became World Catholic Leaders," *Huffington Post Online*, March 1, 2012, http://www.huffingtonpost.com..

2. John L. Allen, Jr., *Cardinal Ratzinger* (New York: The Continuum International Publishing Group, Inc., 2000), 10.

3. Joseph Ratzinger, *Milestones* (San Francisco: Ignatius Press, 1998), 8.

4. Stephen Mansfield, *Pope Benedict XVI: His Life and Mission* (New York: Jeremy P. Tarcher/Penguin, 2005), 25.

5. Ibid., 25.

6. Ibid., 29.

7. Ibid., 32.

8. Ratzinger, *Milestones*, 27.

9. Ibid., 30.

10. George Weigel, *God's Choice: Pope Benedict XVI and the Future of the Catholic Church* (New York: Harper Collins, 2005), 157–158.

11. Ratzinger, *Milestones*, 31–32.

12. Ibid., 33.

13. Weigel, *God's Choice: Pope Benedict XVI and the Future of the Catholic Church*, 163.

14. Georg Ratzinger, *My Brother, The Pope* (San Francisco: Ignatius Press, 2011), 135.

15. Mansfield, *Pope Benedict XVI: His Life and Mission*, 174.

16. Timothy W. Ryback, "Forgiveness," *The New Yorker*, February 6, 2006, *Academic OneFile*, http://go.galegroup.com.ezproxy.denverlibrary.org.

17. Ibid., 66.

18. Ibid., 66.

19. Ibid., 66.

20. Ibid., 66

21. Ibid., 66.

22. Pope Benedict, *Benedict XVI, Light of the World* (San Francisco: Ignatius Press, 2010), 81.

23. Ibid., 81, 82.

24. "Pope Recalls Holocaust as Darkest Period," *America*, September 12, 2005, *Academic OneFile*, http://go.galegroup.com.ezproxy.denverlibrary.org.

25. "Continued Pain Over Kristallnacht," *America*, November 24, 2008, *Academic OneFile*, http://go.galegroup.com.ezproxy.denverlibrary.org.

26. Ratzinger, *My Brother, The Pope*, 14.

27. Michael Collins, *Pope Benedict XVI: The First Five Years* (Dublin, Ireland: The Columba Press, 2010), 92, 93.

Chapter 3

ENTERING THE PRIESTHOOD

When he was just 18 years of age, and just months after being released from the prisoner of war camp, Joseph and his brother, Georg worked to rebuild Saint Michael's Seminary that, for six years, had been used as a military hospital. After the rebuilding was complete, the next step for the brothers' seminarian education was to attend the major seminary at Freising. This school too suffered from war's destruction and it had also served as a military hospital. Due to the building's condition, classes were slow to begin; however, all the students were quite eager to get started. The group of about 120 ranged in age from 18 to almost 40, and many who had been soldiers, for much or all of the war, began a continuation of their studies in anticipation of entering the priesthood. Despite the eagerness of the students to continue what they had begun prior to the war, the circumstances of their life mirrored the life of all Germans at the time. Food was scarce and day-to-day living was difficult, at best. Books were borrowed and classes were held in temporary classrooms. Slowly and steadily, the students began to experience a semblance of familiarity and order. To relieve some of the difficulties and as part of the Christmas festivities in 1945, Joseph and Georg organized a reunion. While the occasion was meant to be a celebration and was a moving experience for the community of seminarians, it was also a stark reminder of how many students were lost in the war.

At the seminary at Freising, the younger seminarians were studying side by side with battle-hardened men who had experienced the terror and atrocities of combat. Many of these men understandably had a somewhat dim view of many of the younger students, as they had not gone through the darkness of war. Later in his life, Cardinal Ratzinger reflected on the mix of students this way, "It was understandable that many of the older combatants looked down on us youngsters as immature children who lacked the sufferings necessary for the priestly ministry . . . since we had not gone through those dark nights that alone can give full shape to the radical assent a priest must give."[1] He wrote, "Despite their differences in ages and their war experiences, they were bound together by a great sense of gratitude for having been allowed to return home from the abyss of those difficult years." He wrote that their appreciation for what they had now "created a common will and bond for everything that had been neglected. They all would now serve Christ in his Church for better times, for a better Germany, and for a better world."[2] Joseph immersed himself in the lessons taught by these embattled men. He endeavored to understand their personal suffering and the knowledge that suffering was essential for a priest to give himself to God. This understanding of hardship stayed with Joseph throughout his life. Despite the differences and the adversities experienced by all of the seminarians, enthusiasm to begin anew flourished within the community.

As a seminarian at Freising, Joseph immersed himself into the seminary community and developed friendships that lasted throughout his life. The music that flowed throughout the school, the theatrical performances, and the liturgical festivities had a lifelong influence on Joseph. It was, however, the Church liturgy and worship that was his anchor. His memories of the seminary cathedral and the hours of prayer in the chapel were strong and remained with him. At this time, Joseph was undergoing an awakening that was perhaps prompted by the trauma of war, or perhaps he was just allowing himself to feel the burdens and the joys of the wider world in a new way. He was now more focused on being human and aware of the dramas of life itself. He was also deeply influenced by the rector at the seminary church, Michael Höck, who was called "the Father" for his affectionate ways and also because he had endured five years at the notoriously dreadful Dachau concentration camp. What he felt about God, he learned while a prisoner in one of the most horrific places known to man. For seminary students, the joy expressed by this man they called "Father" was a true example of a prayerful life and a passion for loving others. It was the example of Father Höck that enhanced the sense of community for all the seminarians in Freising.

In 1947, his two years of the study of philosophy—the curriculum of the time—ended. Joseph asked to continue his studies at the University of Munich and the bishop gave his permission. The next step in Joseph's religious training was to enter a school that also continued to recover from the destruction of the war, and was the gathering place of some of the preeminent theological minds in Germany. It was Joseph's intention to become immersed in the intellectual debates of the time at the university in Munich and be able to dedicate himself to theology as his future profession.

THE UNIVERSITY OF MUNICH

Joseph entered the Herzogliches Gregorianum, the theological institute associated with the University of Munich on September 1, 1947. This school, founded in 1494 by Duke George the Rich for candidates to the priesthood from the whole of Bavaria, offered a rigorous course for clergy intending to pursue a career in academic theology. Just as at Freising, the war had devastated this school and it was, for the most part, ruined. In addition, there was a shortage of fuel for heating, which made a winter semester difficult to manage. Students lived in temporary, cramped quarters and used a library that was inadequate for study. Food remained scarce and the students and faculty could not depend on the fruits of the farmland, as was the case at Freising. Despite the ongoing adversities, Cardinal Ratzinger always remembered his time at the institute fondly, saying it was a time where his early life decisions were formed. He found himself rambling through the school's park, half of which was laid out in the French garden style, and the other half in the English style; here is where he would be deep in thought, where decisions took shape, and where what he heard in the lectures were thought through.

The Nazis had closed the institute in 1938 because Cardinal Faulhaber, the same man who drove into the village square and so impressed
a five-year-old Joseph, had refused to appoint a professor known to have
Nazi sympathies. When it reopened, the faculty had to be rebuilt, with
many of the new faculty coming from institutions of what had been
eastern Germany. Even though the school had temporary quarters,
used borrowed texts, and had cramped living conditions, the faculty
that came together to educate future theologians were theologians in
the fields of Old and New Testaments, Church history, theology, dog-
matism, pastoral theology, and canon law. These would be the experts
guiding young Joseph's educational world and he looked forward to all
the lectures of such renowned theological minds.

As a theological student, Joseph entered a curriculum that included
a study of the Bible and theology at a time when these fields were undergoing changes that would newly define religious thinking. For most
of the past century, studying the Bible included applying the methods
of literary criticism. As a result of this accepted method, the scriptures
themselves were considered to be a product of human invention, written by men writing at a specific time in history with a limited view of
the world, all the while applying a cultural bias to their work. Scholars
of the Munich school attempted to understand the Bible in this way, examining the Bible in the same way as examining the writings of Shake-
speare or any other literary work. This approach was meant to be more
of a scientific inquiry into religion and it was believed that a new world
of religious truth was beginning. However, this method was considered
untruthful to those who regarded the Bible as God's words, and therefore sacred. It was World War I that did away with this method. Some
of the scholars of this era now structured theology from the individual's
viewpoint. What might God mean to the individual in the modern
world? And, if Jesus existed in the first century, might Jesus be of faith
and not of history? These questions permeated among theologians at
the time when Joseph entered the University of Munich's institute.
For Joseph, this meant being a part of a traditional Catholic approach
to faith as well as being a part of new study. Joseph was a man of God,
living in accord with God's life. He intended to be a scholar, bringing
intellectual thinking to the study of the Bible and to the history of the
Catholic Church.

Joseph's favorite among the institute's faculty was Friedrich Wilhelm Maier, professor of New Testament exegesis, the interpretation of religious writings. As a religious scholar, Maier had been a leading proponent of the two-source theory of the first three Gospels. He believed that the Gospel of Mark and other sources were the basis of the Gospels of Matthew and Luke. Catholic tradition, however, holds that Matthew was the earlier Gospel and was, therefore, the primary source.[3] Because his views were outside of the Catholic tradition, Maier had been let go by the Vatican from his professorship of theology prior to World War I, and although he served as a chaplain during the war and later served as a prison chaplain, the sting of his rejection by the Vatican never left him, and by the time he was a faculty member at the institute, he was considered a brilliant theologian and very popular with his students; still, the trauma of his dismissal never left him. For Joseph, his favorite professor was a man of deep faith and a priest who went to great lengths to teach and develop the students entrusted to him. The students were captivated by Maier; because of his popularity, the lecture rooms soon proved to be too small and students had to arrive early to get a seat. Despite the fact that Maier was marked by the Vatican as one who espoused questionable doctrine, Joseph loved him, and he had compassion for what his seminary mentor had been through.

At least some of Joseph's views of orthodoxy, or the accepted beliefs of the Church, could well have come from his time studying with a professor who was also one of his greatest seminarian mentors. Gottlieb Söhngen had once wanted to be a philosopher; as a philosopher, Söhngen had a passion for seeking the truth and for asking questions about the foundation and goal of all considered as authentic. Circumstances later pushed Söhngen toward theology, and even later toward Christianity and to the question about the essence of Christianity. What greatly impressed Joseph was that this professor was never satisfied in theology with the same sort of positivism, or the theory that knowledge is acquired through observation and experimentation. He always asked questions concerning the truth of the matter and questions concerning the immediate reality of what is believed.[4]

It was Söhngen who rejected the view that Mary was taken bodily into heaven at the end of her life. During a debate, a Lutheran friend asked the professor, "But what will you do if the dogma is nevertheless defined? Won't you then have to turn your back on the Catholic Church?" The professor replied in words that resonated with Joseph for the rest of his life, "If the dogma comes, then I will remember that the church is wiser than I and that I must trust her more than my own erudition." Cardinal Ratzinger later summarized the episode this way, "I think that this small scene says everything about the spirit in which theology was done here—both critically and with faith." He had concluded that the wisdom of the Church was to be trusted in the face of all new ideas.[5]

By the fall of 1949, the school was livable and the students and faculty moved from their quarters outside of Munich and into the city itself. In their old quarters, they had all lived closely together, and now they were living and studying in more spacious lodgings. The result was that what was once a sense of a closely knit family seemed now to be lost, but what was gained was that they were living in the city, and they were all able to live and study at what had become a well-rounded university. For Joseph, the time outside of the city and living and studying there was a time of great awakening, a time when he was filled with hope, and had an enormous trust in his fellow students, his professors, and in his choice of the priesthood. Later in his life, when he visited the University of Munich's institute, everything that happened to him in those crucial days easily came back to him.

In the summer of 1950, after his final exams were over, Joseph was invited to participate in a competition for promising theological candidates. The competition's assignment required that the responses be written over a nine-month period and submitted anonymously. For the student winning the competition's prize, there would be a sum of money awarded, and the student would also graduate with a summa cum laude designation. They would also have the opportunity to proceed directly to a program of study leading to a doctorate degree. The topic of the assignment, chosen by one of the faculty members, was "The People and the House of God in Augustine's Doctrine of the Church." Since Augustine and his beliefs formed one of Joseph's favorite topics of study, he was overjoyed to be selected to take part in this competition and was certainly aware of the honor of being asked to compete. Throwing himself into the work, he was soon overwhelmed; besides the work involved, he was also preparing for his ordination as priest—the official installation ceremony into the Catholic priesthood. Already having completed his studies at the University of Munich, he was now under the supervision of the seminary at Freising and was taking courses in practical ministry, including preaching, counseling, and pastoral theology. It was his brother, Georg, who assisted him in getting all of his work completed and helped in taking care of the day-to-day needs so that Joseph could concentrate on his work. Their sister, Maria, also pitched in, using her skills as a legal secretary to help in editing and typing. Completing the competition's assignment just in time, and also completing his preparations for his ordination, Joseph learned that his Augustine project had been chosen and that he would be allowed to work on his doctorate degree at the University of Munich. This honor confirmed what had been known by his professors and colleagues—that Joseph possessed a brilliant theological mind. His life now was focused on the next step of becoming a priest—his official ordination—which promised to be a great celebration for him, for his brother, who would also be entering the priesthood at the same time, and for their family.

At the end of their study at Freising, where they prepared for ordination, Joseph and his brother were ordained on the Feast of Saints Peter and Paul, a traditional day of ordination within the Catholic Church, in Freising Cathedral on June 29, 1951. Cardinal Faulhaber ordained the brothers along with 40 men to the priesthood in the elaborate, moving rite that has been used for centuries in the Catholic Church. Never doubtful, and always the scholar, Joseph wrote in his memoir *Milestones,* "At the moment when the elderly archbishop laid his hands on me, a little bird—perhaps a lark—flew up from the high altar in the cathedral and trilled a little joyful song. And I could not but see in this a reassurance from on high, as if I heard the words 'This is good, you are on the right way.'"[6]

Father Joseph Ratzinger and his brother, Father Georg Ratzinger, offered their first mass on July 8 in the village of Hufschlag, outside of Traunstein, in Bavaria. For any new priest anywhere in the world, a first mass is a time for rejoicing, but for these newly ordained priests, a first mass was especially joyful. For Joseph, it was this auspicious occasion and the days that followed that filled his spirit with overwhelming joy. He knew he had been transformed and marked by God for a special purpose. Yet, he was also keenly aware that it was not about him specifically, but that as a priest, he was a vehicle through which Christ could touch other men and women. This first mass was also an occasion of tremendous pride for the Ratzinger parents. Over 1,000 people attended the mass at their home parish church, Saint Oswald in Traunstein, having arrived on Saturday for the Sunday liturgies. Lights provided a path to the Ratzinger home and a Catholic youth choir sang during the evening. Adding to the weekend's festivities, cannons were fired, and Father Els from their village of Traunstein gave a talk to the crowd of pilgrims that had come to join in the celebration. Early on Sunday, Saint Oswald's Church was overflowing. The two brothers walked the decorated streets to the church, as clergy from neighboring churches and village dignitaries formed a long procession making their way to mass. Joseph led the mass first, and then it was Georg's turn; the cathedral choir sang a composition by Haydn. Joseph's first sermon was a reflection on the five tasks that Cardinal Faulhaber, his mentor and who had ordained Joseph and his brother in early June, had given him—to offer sacrifice, to bless, to preside, to preach, and to baptize. After thanking the congregants, Joseph humbly asked that they help him in carrying out his duties. For their first mass cards, each brother selected scripture verses. For Joseph, it was a line from Corinthians, "We aim not to lord over your faith, but to serve your joy." After mass, with all the songs and saying of the prayers of blessing, the crowd gathered in a local restaurant called the Sailer Keller, where the new priests gave after-dinner speeches. On August 1, Father Joseph Ratzinger was assigned as an assistant pastor in the Parish of the Precious Blood in Munich.

NOTES

1. Stephen Mansfield, *Pope Benedict XVI: His Life and Mission* (New York: Jeremy P. Tarcher/Penguin, 2005), 46.

2. Joseph Ratzinger, *Milestones* (San Francisco: Ignatius Press, 1998), 41, 42.

3. Ibid., 56.

4. Ratzinger, *Milestones*, 55, 56.

5. Mansfield, *Pope Benedict XVI: His Life and Mission*, 58, 59.

6. Ratzinger, *Milestones*, 99.

Chapter 4

PASTORAL MINISTRY, DOCTORATE DEGREE, AND A THEOLOGIAN

PASTORAL MINISTRY

Assistant Pastor at the Parish of the Precious Blood in Munich

Joseph's new assignment to the church in Munich was seemingly the perfect introduction to ministry because the parish was located in a residential suburb of the city where intellectuals, artists, and government officials lived and worshipped alongside household workers and shopkeepers. For this newly ordained priest, it was an opportunity to provide pastoral care to all walks of life in the bustling city of Munich. He was young, eager to serve his flock, and was also idealistic. However, the ministerial load was immense for this new priest. Many of the newly ordained do not fully understand how busy a parish is until it is time to serve. The rectory, where he and other priests lived, was comfortable; yet, it was small and undeniably too hectic for a naturally introverted Joseph. In addition, the workload was overwhelming, with unfamiliar tasks and responsibilities. His schedule included giving 16 hours of varying levels of religious instruction every week; he heard confessions an hour each day, except on Saturday, when he heard confessions continuously for four hours. On Sunday, he celebrated two masses and gave two sermons. Joseph was also responsible for the youth ministry, and was one of the priests who presided over burials, sometimes one per week. Along with all these near constant and growing responsibilities, he also conducted baptisms and weddings.

His model at this time of his pastoral work was the pastor of the parish, Father Blumschein, who gave the rectory its own special character. Blumschein insisted that the priests "glow." This priest was known to give all of himself to his people, Cardinal Ratzinger wrote, and he "glowed" from within. He said Blumschein, "from his last breath, desired with every fiber of his being to offer priestly service. He died, in fact, bringing the sacraments to a dying person. His kindness and inner fervor for his priestly mission were what gave a special character to the rectory; and what seemed to be a terribly hectic rectory was really the expression of a continually readiness to serve." Cardinal Ratzinger wrote that "he was terribly in need of such a role model because of the many tasks and responsibilities assigned to him."[1] Since Father Blumschein did not limit himself, neither did Father Joseph. However, he did have some difficulty with his duties at first, but soon the work became easier and he felt great joy, especially when working with the children in the school and their parents. Joseph gave himself to his ministry, and attempted to live up to the example of Father Blumschein, all the while working towards completing his doctoral degree.

A NEW ASSIGNMENT IN FREISING

Joseph's pastoral ministry was brief. On October 1, 1952, Joseph was given a new assignment at the seminary in Freising, and as often happens to priests called to ministries other than at a parish, the new assignment came with some inner conflicts even though it gave him the time to return to his theological writing and research, his first love. He found that he did suffer from the loss of human contacts and the experiences that pastoral ministry offered him. For a time, he wondered if he should continue in pastoral ministry, where he felt he was needed and where he could provide important services. The feeling of being needed had helped him give all he had to give at the parish, and this gave him special joy in his priesthood in a direct way that he would not experience at his new post at the seminary. While his brother remained a parish priest his whole life, Joseph would never again be a parish priest.

At Freising, his responsibilities included giving lectures to seminary students on various topics, including that of the pastoral aspects of the sacraments—a topic that was fresh in his mind and experience from his work at the parish. He also served in the cathedral, hearing confessions and leading mass. Above all, he worked on his studies for a doctoral degree. The doctoral coursework was extremely difficult, especially for a priest with other demanding responsibilities. The work included demonstrating expertise in eight subjects through oral and written examinations, and preparation for an open debate in which a thesis from all theological disciplines would have to be defended. As difficult and as time consuming as all the preparation was, Joseph excelled in every task, and once again, his mentors realized what an exceptional mind he possessed—a mind greatly influenced by war, depravity, and piousness. In July 1953, Joseph proudly received his doctoral degree in the presence of his brother, mother, and father.

FATHER RATZINGER AS PROFESSOR, THE BEGINNING OF HIS ACADEMIC CAREER

After receiving his doctorate in theology, Joseph's academic career was launched. Along with lecturing at the University of Munich, he began the work on his *Habilitation*, a post-doctoral degree, which qualifies one to hold a chair at a German university, and entails the completion of a scholarly book that proposes a thesis that is defended and approved by an academic committee. It would also confirm him as a serious thinker and possessing a great academic and theological mind. The first decision was what the theme would be for his *Habilitation*. For this, he turned again to his mentor, Gottlieb Söhngen, for help. Since Joseph's prior work was in the area of patristic theology, a work relating to the early Christian writers and to Saint Augustine, it was decided he should turn to the Middle Ages and the thinking of Saint Bonaventure, an Italian medieval scholastic theologian and philosopher. The *Habilitation*, it was decided, would be in fundamental theology—the concept of revelation. In Christianity, revelation is the demonstration of the Divine Will, a showing or revealing of what is believed to be the divine will or truth. Joseph eagerly went to work.

After gathering his materials and perfecting an outline, and with the actual writing of the work yet to begin, Joseph was asked to consider taking a position as the Chair for dogmatic and fundamental theology at the College for Philosophy and Theology in Freising. The faculty at Freising knew of Joseph's work and also knew him personally, and invited him to fill the position. Because he still had to begin writing the main part of the *Habilitation*, he felt it would be extremely difficult to do both the writing and fulfilling the responsibilities as Chair, along with his other day-to-day responsibilities; and because at this point in time, all his responsibilities and opportunities seemed to be moving very fast, he requested a delay in the appointment for a year, which was approved and granted.

By the summer of 1954, Joseph felt he had written enough of the basic outline of his *Habilitation* and was able to accept the Chair for dogmatic and fundamental theology at Freising. Due to the death of one of the elderly professors, an affordable residence became available. He began lecturing in the winter semester that began in October. The next year was an unrelenting schedule of lecturing and writing. Despite the crushing workload, the enthusiastic students were refreshing and inspiring for Joseph. He began a series of lectures on the topic of "God," a lecture class that lasted four hours each week. Through his lecturing, he experienced great enjoyment from working with the students and in moving through the richness of the tradition of church doctrine lectures each week; he found he was able to combine the work of the lectures and of writing the book for his *Habilitation*.

Throughout the spring and summer, he continued his efforts at writing. He employed a typist who, unfortunately, was less than accurate and quite slow. The typist also added to his woes by losing pages, which led to Joseph having to duplicate some of his work. With great relief, by the end of the summer of 1955, the manuscript was completed, and by late fall, he was able to submit the required copies to the faculty in Munich. Initially, the work fell short of what was expected. This was a great blow and was certainly unexpected, especially since the work had been initially accepted enthusiastically by his longtime mentor and advisor, Gottlieb Söhngen, who had even used quotes from Joseph's work in his lectures. Another reader, Professor Schmaus, had put the work aside for some time, due to his extremely busy schedule. At Easter in 1956, Schmaus extended a call for experts in church doctrine (dogma) to attend a congress. Joseph attended the assembly and while it was in session, Schmaus met with Joseph privately and told him he would have to reject his *Habilitation* thesis "because it did not meet the pertinent scholarly standards." He added that more details would follow after the appropriate decision by the faculty.[2]

For Joseph, the world seemed to give way and all his work seemed to be for naught. Another thought that weighed heavily on him at the time was what his parents would think. He had moved his parents from their village outside the city of Traunstein to Freising so they could live near him. What would they say now because of his failure, and would he have to leave Freising in disgrace, as a failure? In addition, all his plans for the future were dependent upon him being a professor of theology. The waiting throughout the summer of 1956 for the faculty's response was extremely difficult. He continued with his lectures and also continued to wonder what had happened, what his shortcomings were, and what he would do next.

Joseph had written his *Habilitation* on the idea of revelation in the thinking of Saint Bonaventure, and from the committee's standpoint, he seemed to be making the case that revelation is not the Bible itself, but instead it is God revealing himself through the Bible. Joseph's thesis rejected the idea that scripture should be called revelation, and maintained, as did Bonaventure, "that revelation is something greater than what is merely written down." This is given by the Spirit, and since the Spirit has been giving revelation for centuries, an understanding of the truth of the Bible requires tradition as well as the immediate work of the Spirit.[3] The committee's decision was that the work sounded too modern; of course, it did not help the matter that one of the committee members was an expert on the topic of Joseph's work and he had not been consulted nor asked by Joseph for guidance, especially considering the new approach to the topic itself. The committee determined that the work should be rejected; however, later, they reconsidered. To rework the book would likely have taken years, and the committee's decision to return the book for further work would have been a severe blow to Joseph as a young professor on the rise. Thankfully, the committee reconsidered and the blow to a promising career was thwarted. On February 21, 1957, the *Habilitation* was accepted. He continued his duties as lecturer, and was then named professor of fundamental theology and dogma at the College of Philosophy and Theology in Freising on January 1, 1958.

The chaotic time Joseph experienced over his book-length work marked him as somewhat of a radical in the theological and academic world. While this made him somewhat infamous with his theology students, to church hierarchy, it gave him a reputation of someone who might bring changes to the Catholic Church, if given the chance. And while his students were enamored with his writings and could have expected to find their professor with more nuanced thoughts and stances, as evidenced by his approach in his *Habilitation*, in his popular lectures, his students found him to be a soft spoken man with a calm demeanor. They knew he was a professor with very strong convictions and was obstinate in seeking and telling the truth and they described him as being the smartest man they had ever known, a priest and professor with a devout, pious reputation, and a man whose life of prayer and worship was acknowledged throughout the campuses where he lectured and served. Joseph found himself quickly rising through the academic and theological worlds, with his reputation soaring as a theologian, lecturer, and a spiritual mentor.

During the turbulent times of writing his *Habilitation*, Joseph had been approached by the dean of the Catholic Theological Faculty in Mainz for taking over the Chair's position in fundamental theology. At the time, Joseph immediately turned down offer, feeling it was not at all the appropriate time to make such a move, especially while being in the midst of his critical work on the *Habilitation*, and being so busy with his lecturing and other connected responsibilities; he also knew he could not do this to his parents, who had moved in with him and away from their village home. Then, in the summer of 1958, he was invited to chair the fundamental theology department in Bonn, the very chair that his teacher and mentor, Söhngen, had always wanted for himself. To Joseph, it was his dream and a long-held ambition to accept such a position. It was also an appropriate time for him to make such an important change in his academic and theological career. To enable him to consider moving to Bonn to live and teach, he had to consider the health and well-being of his elderly parents. Fortunately, another change came for Joseph's brother, Georg, who had been continuing his study of music along with his pastoral duties. In 1957,

Georg ended his studies with the master class at the Munich College of Music and was offered a new position as the teacher of music education at the minor seminary and director of the choir at the Parish of Saint Oswald in Traunstein. Along with these duties, he would also engage in various pastoral duties at the parish. With his new positions, he was given a residence located in the heart of the city, and as a result came the possibility of Georg and Joseph's parents moving back to their beloved Traunstein—something they had wished to do, but had not been appropriate for them due to their age and health conditions. With Georg's support of Joseph's move to Bonn, and his willingness for their parents to move in with him, and also with their parents in full support of Joseph's new opportunity, the changes in all their lives was positive.

The Professor at the University of Bonn

When Father Joseph began his lectures as a professor of fundamental theology at the University of Bonn, he found the lecture hall filled to the brim with eager students. He also found that living in the dormitory with theological students was very positive. This allowed him to participate in the day-to-day activities of the students and he easily developed a strong rapport with the budding theologians. In addition, living in the city of Bonn was exciting. While the city itself and the school still showed the remnants of the ravages of the war, especially in the library collections that remained incomplete, it was still a joy to experience all that the campus and the city had to offer a new professor. The pulse of academic life from students and the faculty, the changes in climate, the sights, smells and the international commerce from the River Rhine, and exploring and enjoying the nearby cities of Cologne and Aachen, and the stimulation of the nearby seminaries and theological colleges, and being close to Belgium and the Netherlands, meant for Joseph that it was a time of new stimulations at every turn. Soon, he and a group of students formed a study group that, with new students regularly joining, continued until 1993. He also formed new and lasting friendships with the theological faculty, and found that having several colleagues from his days in Bavaria made him immediately feel comfortable and he knew at once that his decision to move to Bonn and to the university had been the right one.

Professor Joseph Ratzinger shakes the hands of faithful followers in front of the Ramersdorfer Marienkirche (Church of Mary). (AP Photo/Dieter Endlicher)

Joseph called his first semester at Bonn as "one ongoing honeymoon." Unfortunately, sadness entered his life in August 1958, when his father experienced a mild stroke on a hot summer afternoon as he carried Maria's heavy typewriter to the repair shop. The doctor called it a minor stroke and he recovered well. Carrying on with his busy life, he seemed to experience no further health complications. Then, at Christmas of that year, he gave everyone gifts that were deemed to be more than kind and generous, and the family sensed that the elder Ratzinger felt that Christmas might be his last to enjoy. The next August, he suffered yet another stroke and did not recover quite as well. On Sunday, August 23, taking a walk with Joseph's mother on another hot afternoon, he seemed to be fervently praying, and while stopping briefly at the church, he felt restless. At suppertime, he went outside and collapsed, suffering a serious stroke. Two days later, at the age of 81, he died, with the family at his bedside. Joseph returned to Bonn, sensing that his world was far emptier than before. Despite the sadness from his father's passing, Joseph continued to find joy in his life and his tenure as professor at the University of Bonn. It was not long, however, before there would be still other changes in his academic and theological life.

NOTES

1. Joseph Ratzinger, *Milestones* (San Francisco: Ignatius Press, 1998), 100,101.

2. Ibid., 107.

3. Stephen Mansfield, *Pope Benedict XVI: His Life and Mission* (New York: Jeremy P. Tarcher/Penguin, 2005), 64, 65.

Chapter 5

THE PATH TO ROME

FATHER JOSEPH RATZINGER AND THE SECOND VATICAN COUNCIL, 1962–1965

From the time he began his theological studies at the end of World War II to the moment when he first entered the priesthood, Joseph experienced impressive success within the Catholic Church, both as a professor and as a theologian. In a short period of time, he went from his first post at Freising and on to the University of Bonn. During these years, he developed a wide range of lasting friendships and a vast network of colleagues. By the early 1960s, these friends and colleagues were well-placed within the Catholic Church community. Many became bishops, others became cardinals; still others served as advisors and secretaries to senior high-ranking members of the clergy. There was one friendship that was more than fortuitous; it was one that was part of his launch to a career that led him directly to Rome, and ultimately to his election as Pope Benedict XVI.

As a professor at the University in Bonn, Joseph was part of the Cologne archdiocese. While there, he developed what he called a straightforward and even affectionate understanding with the archbishop of

Cologne, Cardinal Joseph Frings. Their friendship came about in part because of Joseph's longtime friendship with the cardinal's secretary, Hubert Luthe, a friend from his seminary days and who had arranged for Joseph to meet the cardinal. Cardinal Frings was considered a legend in the Catholic Church. He was also one of its most influential voices. The archdiocese of Cologne was one of the most powerful and wealthiest in Europe, which gave Frings immense power. He was well known throughout the world because of his various works in distributing aid to third world countries and serving on other councils and conferences. He had a reputation for being moderate, and when he spoke of changes and reforms, he was listened to. It was also thought he had the personal ear of Pope John XXIII, and upon his election as pope, Frings seemed to know early on, from his time in Rome during the conclave, that a Vatican Council was to be called. When it came true, Frings' reputation as an insider grew. When the time came for the Council to begin, Frings took his personal secretary, Luthe, and Joseph, whom he named as his *peritus*—an official Council theologian—to Rome for the Council.

Blessed Pope John XXIII, who called for the Council, was elected as pope just a month prior to his 77th birthday. He died in 1963, only four-and-a-half years after his election. He was beatified on September 3, 2000. Like Pope Leo XIII, elected in 1878, Pope John XXIII was elected more as a caretaker of the papacy, a pope who would serve in an interim, likely due to his advanced age, his apparent health issues, and also possibly as the result of the long time reign of the previous pope, Pius XII. No one within the church's governing body expected Pope John XXIII to make any changes or to issue significant encyclicals. However, that was not Pope John XXIII's intention. Instead, he stunned the Catholic Church, the curia (the administrative body at the Vatican), and perhaps the world, by calling for a new ecumenical council in 1959. The pope's intent was to resolve issues relating to the Catholic Church's relation to the world and to update the language and presentation of its ancient teachings, all while preserving the faith that had been passed down by the apostles, the very roots of the Catholic Church. At this time, Joseph was a professor at the University of Bonn. He wrote in his memoir that when the Council was called, it "reanimated and, for many, intensified even to the point of euphoria the atmosphere of renewal and hope that had reigned in the Church and in theology since

the end of the First World War despite the perils of the National Socialist era."[1]

It was at the Council, as Joseph said in his memoir *Milestones*, that he
"cannot recount the many encounters that were now granted me . . . cannot report on the meetings with bishops from all continents or on personal conversations with only a few of them," and added that the drama
of the years of the Council would be a prominent part of his memoirs.
He wrote that what the reader should know was the question of what the
Council should begin with, and what its "proximate" tasks should be. He
said that Pope John XXIII had given only a "very wide-ranging description
of his purpose in calling a Council and this left the Fathers with an almost
unlimited freedom to give things concrete shape."[2]

The Second Vatican Council, or Vatican II as it is commonly called,
was the 21st Ecumenical Council of the Catholic Church, and was meant
to address the association between the Catholic Church and the rest of
the world. It was announced by and opened under Pope John XXIII on
October 11, 1962, and closed under Pope Paul VI on December 8, 1965.
There were some 3,000 delegates in attendance, including Catholic
bishops, theologians, and other church officials from around the world.[3]
For Father Joseph Ratzinger, involvement in the Council meant forging
lasting relationships and an assurance that he would continue as a rising
star within the Church community.

The calling of the Council was an attempt to implement reforms and
bring the Church up to date in the modern, rapidly changing world.
Throughout the Church's history, it has been able to absorb reform
movements, with the possible exception of the Reformation in the 16th
century, which many believe was influenced as much by the political situation in Europe as by the power of the Catholic Church. In most business,
government, and religious circles, reform is considered positive and even
healthy; however, such calls are often met with cautiousness. This kind
of response is typical within the Catholic Church because, as with any
reform, someone might lose power. At the time of Vatican II, despite
opposition from some inside the curia, the Council voted on reforms
and the changes resulted in confusion that frightened many within the
Church. Some of the changes implemented were—Catholics were now
allowed to pray with Protestants and attend weddings and funerals in
Protestant churches; priests were encouraged to perform mass facing

the congregation, rather than facing the altar; and priests were allowed to perform mass in languages other than Latin, so that the parishioners could finally understand what was being said throughout the service.[4]

The Second Vatican Council was considered by many to be a revolution within Catholicism. In addition, it was referred to as the Council that forced the Catholic Church to change, and the effects of those changes were deemed as revolutionary, to some, even radical. For many Catholics, the changes were too drastic; to others, the changes were welcome and came with great excitement, believing they brought fresh air to the Church itself. The sparks that the Council created are still felt today, even though the Council closed in 1965. Attempts to restore the Church and Catholicism to what was believed and practiced in the years prior to the Council have failed, in part because many believe that Catholics, especially those who have come of age in the past four decades, no longer recognize the right of the Church's leadership to undo what changes were made.

At the time, Pope John XXIII and the members of the Council felt the Catholic Church had to change. The nostalgia for the Church prior to the Council and a push to return and restore much of the discipline of and by the Church prior to the edicts of the Council has continued throughout the decades. There are also Catholics and leaders within the Church who ardently believe that the Church, since Vatican II, is a great improvement over the old Church. They believe the enthusiasm created by the changes introduced by the Council continues on through Catholic parishes. The Catholic population, even with the trauma and confusion since the 1960s, remains loyal to their Catholic affiliation and is strongly committed to Catholic doctrines, which include the Trinity, Incarnation, the Eucharist, Sacrament, and the Papacy. There are Catholics who do not accept blind obedience as a criterion for moral decision making, or adhere strictly to the edicts of the Church in their daily lives. Still, they remain Catholic and steadfast in their faith.

Joseph, because of his relationship with Cardinal Frings, was selected to be a part of the preparations for the Council, which took more than two years. He was asked to comment on and make suggestions to the texts that were sent to the Council committees for discussion. This was a great honor. When the Council commenced, he was included, along with the cardinal's secretary, Father Luthe, on the trip to Rome for the Council meetings, serving as theological adviser to the cardinal, which was yet another great honor, and one that was only part of what propelled him to various offices and advancements within the Church hierarchy, and to later being elected as pope. At the time, Joseph was just 35 years old and had been a theologian for less than a decade; yet, he was able to play a significant role in one of the most pivotal events within the Church in the 20th century.

THE INFLUENCE ON AND THE INFLUENCES OF FATHER JOSEPH RATZINGER OF VATICAN II

The Second Vatican Council has been called the most important religious event of the 20th century and the entire Catholic community around the world anticipated its conclusions. Joseph, and the others who also would be *periti*, theological experts and advisers, certainly looked forward to the opportunities in attending such an epic event. Joseph recognized the strains between those concerned with pastoral care and the scholars, and he looked forward to the discussions brought forth as a result of the pre-Council documents, which he had a part in preparing. While in Rome, Joseph and his good friend, Luthe, lived in a residence for German priests and seminarians near the Piazzo Navona. At the residence and also during the Council, Joseph met with influential theologians and historians. Having such a prominent place at the Council was an inspiration for Joseph and it was here that he engaged in dialogues with great men of the Catholic faith, had a part in history, and furthered his own study in theology.

At the Council, it was Joseph's role as the advisor to Frings to only respond when asked a specific question. However, he did not simply act behind the scenes. Everyone knew of him and while he did not actually speak on the Council floor, he was a public figure. He had lectured on Council topics at various venues in Rome and in Germany, and he organized briefing sessions for the attendees. He also published well-known Council commentaries. While he was not supposed to give opinions in his answers and was to remain objective when responding to questions, he and the other *periti* did not always honor these directives. The Council Fathers openly listened to and responded to the convictions of these advisers and these responses and opinions were believed to set the course and the outcomes of the Council. Joseph already had the ear of and was one of the key sources of the bishops before the first day of the Council on October 10, 1962. He was also a part of the group of German, Austrian, and Luxembourg bishops who met at the priests' residence when they discussed their strategies. Joseph gave the main talk and was essential in forming the first impressions of the German-speaking bishops who represented an influential block at the Council.

During the third session of the Council in 1964, Joseph was asked to serve as a member on the editorial committee, whose purpose was to redraft a decree on missionary activity. The decree was extended into the fourth session, and his mentor, Frings, then supported the document on the floor of the Council. Joseph also worked on the "Word of God" document, where he exercised great personal influence during the last session in 1965. He also worked on the "Dogmatic Constitution of the Church," the doctrine of the Church that was based on scripture and endeavored to restore the balance between the pope and the bishops; many felt this had been lost during the discussions at Vatican I. Joseph's work on these issues were part of the changes imposed by Vatican II, including changes to Church liturgy and how mass was celebrated in countries and cultures throughout the world, the role of the Holy Office, the theory of bishop collegiality, which holds that they are jointly the successors of the original Twelve Apostles, ecumenism, and the Church's role in relations with other Christian churches, and elevated him even further to the level of one of the most important theologians of his time and greatly contributed to his meteoric rise within the Catholic Church and in the eyes of the Vatican in Rome.

While Joseph had very personal experiences at the Council and he was clearly inspired by what took place there for many years after, it is not particularly clear whether his thinking has changed today. Journalist Vittorio Messori in his work, *The Ratzinger Report*, has written that as cardinal, Joseph discussed whether or not he had changed his views since the Vatican Council, as he has been accused of turning from a progressive to an archconservative. His former friend, the liberal-thinking German theologian Hans Kung, said of Joseph's turn to the right as selling his soul for power. In response, Joseph has said of this charge, "It is not I who have changed, but others. At our very first meetings I point out two prerequisites to my colleagues. The first one: our group must not lapse into any kind of sectarianism or arrogance, as if we were the new, the true church . . . with a monopoly on the truth of Christianity. The second one: discussion has to be conducted without any individualist flights forward, in confrontation with the reality of Vatican II with the true letter and the true spirit of the council. . . . I have always tried to remain true to Vatican II, to this *today* of the church, without any longing for a *yesterday* irretrievably gone with the wind and without any impatient thrust toward a *tomorrow* that is not ours."[5]

The Second Vatican Council opened in 1962 and closed in 1965. For all the work completed at the Council, the outcomes are still felt today in churches throughout the world. Among Catholic theologians, the consensus seems to be that it is the commentaries on Vatican II written by then Joseph Ratzinger that are still read today, and are likely to be read for many years to come. They reflect the thinking of the fathers at the Council and provide insights into why the important changes were put forth and implemented.

THE UNIVERSITY OF MÜNSTER

In the summer of 1963, Joseph left the Council, feeling optimistic about what had been accomplished and somewhat pessimistic about the work ahead. It was true that one of the goals of the Council was to breathe new life into the Church, and it was also true that communicating the changes to be implemented in churches around the world could prove difficult. There was still much work to be done and when Joseph left Rome, there were still two more years of work to be completed. In the midst of all this was yet another critical decision to be made. Joseph was glad to be returning to the University of Bonn; he loved his students and also loved the Rhineland, and because of the continuing influence of Cardinal Frings, he was anxious to continue his work. However, a good friend and the dogma specialist at the University of Münster, Hermann Volk, was made bishop of Mainz in 1962, and his university chair was vacant. Joseph received the call to consider moving to Münster and taking the chair, providing the university with his dogma expertise. Bishop Volk pressured Joseph and his friends advised him that dogma was the correct path for him to take in his theology career because it would open a wider sphere of influence than the path of fundamental theology, as at Bonn. While the arguments appeared simple and accurate, for Joseph, the decision was not at all simple. After a great deal of thought and some vacillation, he made the difficult decision to decline the offer at Münster. Like many difficult decisions, the offer remained at the back of his mind, especially as the faculty at Bonn was in turmoil over the failing of two doctoral dissertations, which would decide the fates of two young scholars. Remembering the drama surrounding his own dissertation, the decision to rethink the offer became clear. He knew he could assist the two young scholars and it was clearly providence that was pointing the way to Münster. He also knew that a greater involvement in the area of dogma, which he had previously discounted, was the right theological path. After discussing the whole of the situation with Cardinal Frings, he accepted the offer and took the post at the University of Münster. The move turned out to be the right one. The faculty and his new colleagues sincerely accepted him and the facility itself fit his personal needs. He did miss Bonn, however, as he had truly enjoyed the city, the river, the intellectual dynamics, and certainly, the students that were so important to his work.

In the early 1960s, there were many changes in Joseph's life. His work at the Council continued, splitting his time between the university and Rome. The move to his new post continued to be positive and his work there was satisfying. He knew that he had made the correct decision to move from the area of fundamental theology to that of dogma. Unfortunately, yet another occurrence that year deeply affected him. His brother, Georg, noticed that their mother had not been feeling well and had been eating less and less. By August of 1963, her physician gave the sad and difficult diagnosis of stomach cancer. While being treated, she continued to keep house for Georg until the end of October, when her health took yet another turn and she collapsed. Through her increasing pain and while being confined to her bed, she continued to be positive and was yet another example of strength and love for her family. In mid-December, she died. Joseph wrote of her passing that "the radiance of her goodness has remained, and for me it has become more and more a confirmation of the faith by which she had allowed herself to be formed. I know of no more convincing proof for the faith than precisely the pure and unalloyed humanity that the faith allowed to mature in my parents and in so many other persons I have had the privilege to encounter."[6]

THE UNIVERSITY OF TÜBINGEN

In February 1964, not long after their mother's death, Joseph's brother, Georg, took a new position in Regensburg, Germany. This meant there were no family members left in their beloved home town of Traunstein. Now, it was Regensburg, on the River Danube, where Joseph would go for vacations and to visit Georg. Over time, both brothers came to feel at home in the old city. Joseph continued to lecture at the university in Münster and divided his time between there and Rome, as work on the Council continued.

When he returned from the first session of the Council, he felt joyful about the new beginnings in the Church. It was not long, however, that he became deeply troubled by the changes in the climate within the Church itself; he found the mood among the theologians to be troubled. Many believed that there was nothing stable in the Church and everything was open to being revised. Resentment grew towards Rome, to the members of the Council, and to the curia. Other changes were happening as well. When Joseph had arrived in Münster, he was welcomed by his colleagues and by his students. He felt at home in the city and it was not long before he called it his home. He did miss Bavaria, however, where he had deep, long-lasting bonds. It seemed that constantly, there was tug to the more southern part of Germany, where he had been raised and where he and his family had lived for so many years. Fortunately, an offer presented itself to move yet again to another university, this time to the University of Tübingen, which had offered him a position as Chair in fundamental theology in 1959. An offer to join the faculty there was made once again in 1966, except now it was for a second Chair in dogma. Southern Germany beckoned and Joseph accepted the new post, which began in the summer semester of 1966.

Joseph's health at the time was poor, mainly due to the stress of his work at the Council, which closed in December 1965, and also due to the stresses of the initial commute between his post at Münster and his new post at Tübingen. Fortunately, his health improved as the stresses lessened and the charm of the city of Tübingen worked on him. With the exception of his personal accommodations not quite to his liking as they were rather sparse and small, especially compared to his home in Münster, which was luxurious in comparison, he began to thoroughly enjoy his new post and the city itself.

Joseph remained positive about what had been accomplished at Vatican II, and he was enthusiastic about his colleagues at Tübingen, especially those he considered to be "superstars" of German theology, particularly Hans Küng, the dean of Catholic theology faculty, who had offered the new position of Chair in dogma to Joseph without considering any other individuals to fill the position. Joseph was his only suggestion. Joseph and Dean Küng worked closely together and got along very well. They formed a standing Thursday evening dinner engagement where they discussed a journal they edited together; Küng became the only colleague Joseph regularly socialized with. Together, the two men formed a partnership even though they were quite different individuals. Though the two theologians were solidly connected, their contrast was evident, even to the point of Joseph riding around on his bicycle, wearing his professor beret, while Küng, using a fast Alfa-Romeo automobile, quickly moving from one place to another. Another apparent difference was Küng's progressive theology, which was different from Joseph's increasingly conservative theological instincts.

At Tübingen, Joseph continued his work and found his students to be eager listeners. In 1967, Hans Küng was still responsible for the dogma lectures, which left Joseph relatively free to work on a project that he had been pondering for several years. He had developed a series of lectures with the title of "Introduction to Christianity" for students of all disciplines. Out of these lectures came a book of the same name. With an increasing conservative outlook, and finding himself to often be in conflict with many of his colleagues over the direction of the teaching of theology, Joseph made the difficult decision to leave the University of Tübingen after teaching there for three years.

THE UNIVERSITY OF REGENSBURG

In the years following the Second Vatican Council, Joseph was a professor at two prestigious institutions in Munster and Tübingen. He also published his book *Introduction to Christianity*, considered by many to be one of his greatest works. While he had hoped to settle into a period of quiet work at the university in Tübingen, being tired of moving from one place to another, the climate there had changed enough for him to consider moving yet again. In 1967, Bavaria created its fourth university in the city of Regensburg. Initially, Joseph had been considered to be the Chair for dogma, with the responsibility of teaching the set of beliefs held by the Catholic Church; however, he had refused the appointment, hoping to stay in Tübingen. His former colleague and native of Regensburg, Johann Auer, accepted the post. He was again approached for the position when a second Chair was established, and in 1969, he received a formal invitation, which he accepted. His brother, Georg, was also working in Regensburg and that was an additional benefit to the position, even though it entailed yet another move. At the University of Regensburg, he was a professor for the longest time of his academic career. It was also in 1969 that Pope Paul VI appointed Joseph to the International Papal Theological Commission. It was the intention of the Commission to implement the Second Vatican Council's documents. As part of his new post at Regensburg and serving on the Commission, Joseph met one of his greatest friends and colleagues in the debates of the Commission, Hans Urs von Balthasar.

Joseph hoped that the move to Regensburg would be his last. However, the beginning of his new post was not easy. The university had only been created about two years earlier and some of the buildings were still being constructed. Joseph's work took place in a building that had part of the monastery of the Dominicans in Regensburg. With a cloister, or covered outdoor walkways, and winding halls, it was also attached to a gothic Dominican church, all of which lent a special atmosphere to the students studying theology. The university continued to develop and was able to attract more professors over time. Students continued to arrive at the new university to study law, philosophy, and the natural sciences, along with theology. For Joseph, his circle of doctoral candidates became more international and varied in their theological points of view. His work thrived, partly because of the exchanges of ideas at the university, and because there was never a shortage of controversies that continued to arise.

During his first years at Regensburg, there were several events that proved to be a catalyst in Joseph's career. The first was his appointment to the International Papal Theological Commission established by Pope Paul VI. Most of the members of the Commission had been part of the Second Vatican Council. A second event was what turned out to be his lifelong friendship with Balthasar, a friend he described as someone "with such a comprehensive theological and humanistic education."[7] Another event was the idea, and subsequently the publishing, of the international journal *Communio*. The initial idea of the journal was to promote the communion of sacrament and faith. The journal was eventually published in Germany and Italy. It was edited in partnership with lay individuals who were knowledgeable of both cultures. Eventually, *Communio* was published in 16 languages and became an instrument for theological and cultural discussions.

Yet another event that influenced Joseph while at the university was the publication of the *Missal of Paul VI*. The previous missal, known as a book that contains the prayers, responses, and hymns used in a Catholic mass, had been issued by Pope Pius V in 1570, after the Council of Trent. Some 400 years later, and after another Council, another missal was produced. Joseph was pleased about a new missal as he thought of it as a required liturgical text; however, he was not pleased that the old missal was not to be used any longer, mainly because it had been continuously revised over the centuries and to replace it, he felt, was not respecting the Church's liturgy and its important history. He felt the liturgical innovations in the new missal often went too far.

The years as a professor at the University of Regensburg were prolific. While at the university, he started work on two significant projects. The first was a book on dogmatic theology. When the first author suspended his work on the book due to personal heavy commitments, he suggested that Joseph take over the writing and research. The condition for Joseph's acceptance was that a co-author be added, and one of his colleagues was named. After a considerable amount of work was completed, Joseph had to give up the writing due to his work on the Vatican Council. After the work there ended, Joseph thought he now had the time to resume the work on the book; however, he was then asked to co-author another work—a new, small paperback version of a dogmatic theology book.

While at Regensburg, Joseph built a small house for himself and his sister. The house and its garden were also a place for his brother to visit and a place where his family could be together. For Georg, his work as a music director received international recognition and the Cathedral Choir was also distinguished with great honors.

THE ARCHBISHOP OF MUNICH AND FREISING

In July 1976, the archbishop of Munich, Cardinal Döpfner suddenly died. Joseph was greatly troubled by this news. As he grieved for the cardinal's passing, his sorrow was soon interrupted, first by rumors, and then by more certain news that he was being considered as the cardinal's successor. For Joseph, his own health condition at the time made him believe he would not be a candidate. Besides, he was thought of in the Church's hierarchy as a great scholar and not as someone with

Newly nominated Archbishop of Munich and Freising, Joseph Ratzinger, right, walks with Bishop Ernst Tewes in front of the cathedral of Freising in 1977. (AP Photo/Dieter Endlicher)

experience in governing and administration—both the tasks of an archbishop. He felt his responsibilities within the academic community, as a result of all his years and great successes at universities, were far from that of the responsibilities and qualifications of a bishop. To his great surprise, he was given a letter and was asked to consider it carefully. The letter contained the appointment as archbishop of Munich and Freising, signed by Pope Paul VI. He was tempted to refuse the offer and was in turmoil over what he should do.

After considering his own limitations and what he would bring to the post, and after consulting with Professor Auer, his confessor and mentor, who he expected to tell him to decline the offer, he was greatly surprised when he was encouraged to accept. After a great deal of thought, prayer, and discussions with his mentors, he wrote his acceptance letter. On March 24, 1977, Pope Paul VI appointed Father Joseph Ratzinger as archbishop of Munich and Freising. As archbishop, Joseph chose as his episcopal motto, which all bishops include on their coats of arms, *Cooperatores Veritatis*, or "Co-worker of the Truth." With the assistance of auxiliary bishops, Joseph worked steadily, carrying out his duties with the priests in his archdiocese. Just a few months later, on June 27, 1977, he was elevated to the rank of cardinal in the consistory, the assembly of cardinals and pope, and was ordained on Pentecost Sunday. Joseph's rapid rise in the hierarchy of the Church continued.

MORE CHANGES YET TO COME

While on holiday in Austria in August 1978, word came that Pope Paul VI had died. He had reigned since 1963. As one of the youngest cardinal-electors, Joseph participated in the papal conclave to elect a new pope. On August 26, Albino Luciani, Patriarch of Venice, was elected and took the name Pope John Paul I. While on a trip to Ecuador, Joseph received word that the new pope had suddenly died, after reigning only 33 days. Joseph again traveled to Rome in October for the conclave to elect yet another new pope.

When Pope Paul VI died in 1978, Joseph was on several cardinals' short list to be the next pope. He was also considered at the conclave in October, following the shocking, untimely death of Pope John

Paul I, when Cardinal Karol Wojtyla was elected as pope. Joseph and Karol were close in age, both were considered to be intelligent conservatives, and neither man was Italian. Joseph's career by the time of the conclave in October 1978 was well-known to the assembled cardinals. He was also known for his long academic and theological career and as a priest who was active in the three-year council meetings and decisions, and had, from the outset, supported the changes imposed by the Second Vatican Council. He was also a cardinal who had subsequently changed his mind and did not accept what the Council imposed. On the one hand, for some of the cardinals in the conclave, this initial belief and the later change in what he believed in was a concern.

On the other hand, Cardinal Karol Wojtyla was much less well-known, having served the Church and living in the closed-off society under the rule of the communists in Poland. After several ballots, with Joseph playing a major role in delivering the German vote, and being a major campaigner for the election of his friend since Vatican II, the cardinal from Poland, Karol Wojtyla, was elected pope on October 16, 1978, taking the name Pope John Paul II.

Pope John Paul II wasted little time in showing his great interest in Joseph Ratzinger, the cardinal from Germany. Telling him he wanted Joseph to live and serve in Rome, he offered him the position of the prefect of the Sacred Congregation for the Doctrine of the Faith. Joseph, however, turned down the post, stating it was too soon for him to leave Munich. In 1980, John Paul II named Joseph the *relator*, the person who would be in charge of and provide an account for the proceedings of the Synod of the Family. In this capacity, Joseph managed the synod's activities and prepared reports to be given to the pope. The topic of the report was "The Family" and the contentious subject of birth control was discussed; the bishops, attending from all over the world, had the opportunity to voice their feelings about this topic to the pope. Another topic discussed by the synod was that of virginity before marriage and heterosexual monogamy. Joseph was able to synthesize the many and differing points of view on all the discussed topics. By all accounts, Joseph's handling of the synod was positive and his time as *relator*, at the appointment by the new pope, was successful.

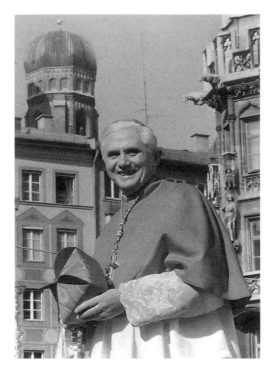

*With the cupolas of Munich's
cathedral behind him, Cardinal
Joseph Ratzinger says farewell
to the Bavarian believers in
Munich in 1982. (AP Photo/
Diether Endlicher)*

As a cardinal, Joseph was at John Paul II's side when the pope flew to Poland in June 1979 to celebrate mass at Nowy Targ, a town in southern Poland. In 1981, when the Polish Communists imposed martial law, Joseph, along with approximately 1,500 people, joined in a protest rally in Munich, along with the leader of the Bavarian wing of the conservative Christian Democrats. In November 1980, the pope traveled to Bavaria. Prior to the trip, Joseph prepared his diocese for the pope's visit, planning the scope and breadth of the trip. There were several glitches in the planned itinerary, including who would be a part of the speeches and what the topics of the speeches that the pope would hear would be, and who would be involved in the meetings with the pope. Despite the bitterly cold weather for the open air mass and these glitches, the visit was considered to be very successful.

For Cardinal Ratzinger, serving his longtime friend, Pope John Paul II, from the beginning of the papacy was certainly fortuitous. John Paul II asked Joseph yet again to serve in the extremely important and certainly vital position of Prefect of the Sacred Congregation for the Doctrine of the Faith. This time, Joseph accepted.

NOTES

1. Joseph Ratzinger, *Milestones* (San Francisco: Ignatius Press, 1998), 120.

2. Ibid., 121, 122.

3. "The Writer's Almanac," *National Public Radio*, October 11, 2010, http://writersalmanac.publicradio.org.

4. Ibid.

5. Greg Tobin, *Holy Father: Pope Benedict XVI Pontiff for a New Era* (New York: Sterling Publishing Co., Inc., 2005), 98, 99.

6. Ratzinger, *Milestones*, 131.

7. Ibid., 143.

Chapter 6

THE PREFECT OF THE CONGREGATION FOR THE DOCTRINE OF THE FAITH

During his long pontificate, John Paul II had many trusted individuals at his side; however, there were few as devoted as Cardinal Joseph Ratzinger. For John Paul II, it was difficult to imagine being pope without Joseph, his friend since the Second Vatican Council, and one of his principal curial advisors. Not long after John Paul II was established at the Vatican, it was clear that Joseph was now one of the most powerful leaders of the Catholic Church.

Two years after becoming pope, John Paul II decided to visit Germany. One stop on his journey was Munich. His host there was his longtime friend, Cardinal Joseph Ratzinger. One year later, and for the second time, Joseph was summoned to Rome for the position of Prefect of the Congregation for the Doctrine of the Faith (CDF). At first, Joseph hesitated. The change meant leaving Munich as archbishop, and he felt it was not the right time to leave his diocese. He did not feel that as a theologian, he should judge the works of other theologians—something he would do as prefect. It also meant abandoning his hope of writing his theological masterpiece. He said, "For me, the cost was that I couldn't do full time what I had envisaged for myself, namely, really contributing my thinking and speaking to the great intellectual conversation of our time, by developing an opus of my own."[1]

John Paul II would not relent and Joseph finally agreed. Together, with his sister, Maria, who was keeping house for him in Munich, he moved to Rome. This Vatican position, one that popes personally appoint, was important because it involved interpreting Catholic modern thought, and for this, John Paul II determined he would rely on the well-known German academic and theologian Cardinal Joseph Ratzinger. After being asked twice, Joseph accepted the appointment and until April 2, 2005, he served as prefect of the Congregation. As the longest-serving prefect, he was called the "Grand Inquisitor," "the Enforcer," "God's Rottweiler," and even "the Panzer Cardinal," a reference to Joseph's service in the German Army during World War II. His Congregation for the Doctrine of the Faith was referred to as "God's Gestapo" and the "Headquarters of the Thought Police."[2] The Congregation was also formerly known as the Inquisition. On accepting the position, Joseph said that "the CDF meant spending the bulk of [his] time on the little and various things that pertain to factual conflicts and events." It also meant giving up the scholar-bishop's luxury of seizing intellectual opportunities. He put it this way, "I had to free myself from the idea that I absolutely have to write or read this or that."[3]

The history of the Congregation, known first as the Holy Office, dates back to 1542, when the pope, believing that heresy was rampant, gave the charge of dealing with doctrinal matters to a set of six cardinals. The present form of the Holy Office within the Vatican came in 1965, when Pope Paul VI renamed it the Congregation for the Doctrine of the Faith. It was again reformed in 2001, when Pope John Paul II modified it once again. Presided over by a Cardinal Prefect, the Congregation governs anything having to do with the content of the Catholic faith. It is also known for disciplining theologians whose teachings are judged to be incompatible with the Catholic faith. It examines cases such as apparitions, admission to or expulsion from the ministry, the imposition and removal of the ban of excommunication, the setting up or closing of religious orders, offenses against the Catholic faith, and abuses of the celebration of the sacraments. All documents prepared by Vatican offices, including those prepared for or by the pope, pass through this office to be examined, ensuring that there is no hint of heresy or anything that might cause confusion. Two other offices presided over by the prefect are the International Theological Committee, which deals with theological developments, and the International Biblical Commission, which examines insights and advances in biblical scholarship. The vaults within this office contain archives of documents that date back to the 16th century; other documents are kept in the Vatican's secret archives located near the Vatican galleries. The Congregation's office also houses books and journals for the office's work. It was within this office that Joseph took residence in early 1982. At the pope's side as prefect, Joseph continued to be one of his closest advisers in the administrative body of the Vatican. Joseph was assisted by a secretary and other administrators on a daily basis, and there were also external advisors and consultants who helped in reviewing and preparing documents. Despite an internal and external staff, there was an intense and constant workload, and several times, Joseph requested additional assistance and even asked to be relieved of the position and allowed to retire. While his requests were always considered, he was encouraged to continue his work. Diligently, Joseph continued to carry out his many responsibilities, which included working faithfully with his eminence, Pope John Paul II.

By appointing Joseph as prefect of the CDF, it meant that the pope took theology very seriously. Instead of appointing a Church bureaucrat to the office, John Paul II chose someone whom everyone within the Church regarded as an unparalleled scholar and someone regarded as possessing one of the finest theological minds of the century. At the pope's direction and with Joseph as prefect, there would be a wide-ranging discussion on theology. As a close advisor and the pope's prefect, Joseph and John Paul II met weekly to review the work of the CDF; Joseph was also a part of the pope's regularly scheduled luncheons for the purpose of discussing his general audience addresses. These luncheons were also important for shaping the teaching documents, including the pope's encyclicals.

John Paul II's confidence in Joseph as prefect of CDF extended beyond their conversations about theology and doctrinal matters. They also included discussions on the nature and exercise of the pope's own papal authority. John Paul II wanted Joseph to be involved in aspects of the Church's governance. As a result, Joseph was a member of five Vatican congregations—Oriental Churches, Divine Worship, Bishops,

Evangelization of Peoples, and Catholic Education. He was also a member of the pontifical council, Christian Unity, and two pontifical commissions—one for Latin America and another for the reconciliation of the Lefebvrist schismatics; he was also a member of the advisory council of the Second Section of the Secretariat of State, known as the Vatican "foreign ministry." By these many appointments, John Paul II ensured that Joseph would be a regular presence in the most important discussions of the Vatican. Joseph was also elevated to the highest title a cardinal can receive, that of titular Bishop of Ostia in 2002. This elevation came after his fellow cardinal bishops elected Joseph as dean of the College of Cardinals.[4]

The CDF's charge was that of promoting theology in the Church as well as safeguarding Catholic doctrine. Doctrinal integrity is spelled out in *Pastor Bonus* (meaning The Good Shepherd) and is known as the 1988 apostolic constitution. This document makes the CDF the last stop in the Vatican for the issues within the Church, including that of reviewing the work of theologians who may have moved away from the Church's accepted views, and disciplining them. During Joseph's term as prefect, the congregation met these responsibilities and promoted the development of theology through a number of important documents.

A significant publication was issued in 1982, the revised Code of Canon Law and the Catechism of the Catholic Church, with assorted editions and languages throughout the 1990s. One of the first controversial documents Joseph, as prefect, signed was the notification confirming the excommunication of Archbishop Pierre Martin Ngo Dinh Thuc, formerly bishop of Hue in Vietnam. For over a century, the Vatican had reserved the right to appoint bishops to dioceses throughout the world. As archbishop, Dinh Thuc participated in the ordination of priests and bishops without the approval of the Holy See. Dinh Thuc, viewed as a traditionalist, had refused to accept what the Second Vatican Council imposed and had known the French Archbishop Marcel Lefebvre, who had founded a traditionalist seminary at Ecône in Switzerland. At this seminary, students prepared for the priesthood according to the norms applied prior to Vatican II. In addition, Archbishop Thuc had travelled to Spain to ordain those known as breakaway clerics, including an anti-Pope, Gregory XVIII. When the Vatican was informed of the consecration in violation of canon law, Joseph, as prefect, and the Congregation were obliged to confirm his automatic sentence of excommunication. Thuc later repented his action and the sentence was lifted; however, shortly thereafter, he continued his activities, and a renewed excommunication was enacted. Prior to his death in 1984, Thuc reconciled with the Church and received a special blessing from Pope John Paul II. During this time, the Congregation maintained a dialogue with the traditionalist community headed by Archbishop Lefebvre, and Joseph found that privately, he was in sympathy with many of Archbishop Lefebvre's complaints. It was his particular love of Church liturgy that made him a supporter of its role within the Church, and he was dismayed by what the Second Vatican Council had done to strip Church liturgy from its ornate excesses, even though he had argued for changes to Church liturgy while serving as a theologian at Vatican II.

Another case for the prefect and the CDF was the Boff case. A Brazilian Franciscan, Leonardo Boff, wrote his doctoral dissertation in Germany in the late 1960s with then Professor Joseph Ratzinger as one of his readers. In 1981, in his book *Church: Charisma and Power*, Boff applied a method inspired by Marxism to the nature and structure of the Catholic Church. He concluded that the ordained hierarchy of bishops and priests was a "sinful social structure" of which the Church should rid itself. The Catholic Church's view on the hierarchy is that it is the will of Christ and is a fundamental part of Christ's constitution of the Church. Boff's writings made it clear that he did not believe in nor would teach this Church belief. As a result, the CDF issued a letter on the book in 1985, stating that the book was doctrinally deficient. The CDF insisted that Boff maintain a year of silence on the subjects that the CDF found the book to be deficient in. Boff's writings then could be more thoroughly examined, and Joseph, as prefect of the CDF, agreed to the imposed year of silence. The decisions on the Boff case were met with a great deal of criticism by members of religious orders, including Brazilian bishops. For his part, while Joseph maintained affection for his former student, he was the target of most of the criticism. Boff eventually left the Church, and controversies briefly emerged again during the time between the death of John Paul II and the election of his former professor as pope.

Another case that thrust Joseph as prefect into the limelight in the United States was the Curran case. Father Charles Curran had been a symbol of Catholic theological dissent in the United States since his time as a junior professor at the Catholic University of America, when he helped to accelerate Catholic teachings on the appropriate means of family planning, according to an encyclical issued by Pope Paul VI in 1968. Since that time, Father Curran published articles and books that questioned the Church's teachings on sexual ethics. The CDF became involved in the Curran case and their observations detailed the points in which Curran referred to the Church's teachings as being false. Curran would not change his teaching and writing to conform with the settled teaching of the Church; the CDF notified him that in his post of priest and theologian at a Catholic institution of higher learning, he must conform to the views of the Church. After discussions between Curran and the CDF in Rome, Curran stated that he would not bring his teaching and writing into conformity with that of the Church and proposed a compromise in which he would retain his tenure at the university and continue to teach moral theology, but not on the topic of sexual ethics. This proposed compromise was not deemed as acceptable by the CDF, and in a letter from Cardinal Ratzinger to the cardinal and chancellor of Catholic University, he wrote that Father Curran "was no longer . . . considered suitable (or) eligible to exercise the function of a Professor of Catholic Theology." Curran was suspended from the university faculty. After negotiations failed in an out-of-court settlement, the case went to trial and Curran lost. He then accepted a chair at Southern Methodist University in Dallas, Texas. Father Curran was not suspended from the priesthood and was not forbidden to publish; he was not barred from making public appearances or from lecturing. In his response to the observations made by the CDF, Father Curran stated that he did not believe to be true what the Catholic Church taught, and that he did not intend to teach what the Catholic Church taught on the issues of sexual morality. One aspect of the Curran case that came to light was that what Vatican II imposed and what the pope and Cardinal Ratzinger believed was a different understanding of Catholic teaching than what Father Curran and others of his same beliefs did. Besides, the case also touched on the future of the Church. Curran was believed to be a priest who had a genuine pastoral decency and was convinced that lowering the Church's moral expectations and altering its moral teachings was an appropriate response to what the lives of most human beings experience in their own sexual integrity.[5] The Curran case brought Joseph as prefect of the CDF into the limelight within the Catholic community in America. The case polarized conservatives and progressives. Those sympathetic to the cardinal believed that he was doing what the pope himself expected and was acting in his role as protector of the pope. There were some, however, who began to feel the prefect was a merciless enforcer of the law.

Another case for the CDF and the prefect was one that involved the writings of Dominican Father Edward Schillebeeckx. The CDF sent a notification to the Father regarding his book *The Church With a Human Face: A New and Expanded Theology of Ministry*. The problems identified in the book concerned the ordination of women and the celebration of the Eucharist. Schillebeeckx was considered one of the most scholarly theologians of the 20th century and any move by the Vatican against this Belgian-born priest was thought to have serious consequences. This time, the CDF limited their notification to noting the "deficient" character of the book. Since Schillebeeckx had retired from teaching, the matter of his writings died down quickly, although another reason for its swift resolution may have been the significance of a document published two weeks later in 1976 by the CDF and Prefect Ratzinger, entitled *Letter to the Bishops of the Catholic Church on the Pastoral Care of Homosexual Persons*. It was addressed to the bishops of the church; yet, it received wider publicity than any other document published with the signature of the prefect.

In America, just weeks earlier, the Apostolic Visitation in the Archdiocese of Seattle had come to a close. The archbishop had been informed that one investigation would take place; instead, there were two. The first was led by Archbishop James Hickey, and the second was led by Cardinal John O'Connor of New York, Cardinal Joseph Bernardin of Chicago, and Archbishop John Quinn of San Francisco. As a result of the inquiries, Archbishop Hunthausen of Seattle was told to temporarily hand over his control of his administration to the auxiliary bishop, Donald Wuerl. The cause of this action was the archbishop's care for homosexual people in Seattle. The Vatican expected a clear declaration that although homosexuality was not evil, homosexual activity was immoral and contrary to biblical evidence. While the document from the CDF had acknowledged that any kind of discrimination was wrong, it also noted that biblical evidence and the tradition of the Church was clearly opposed to homosexual activity and regarded it as immoral. The issue of sexuality was not to go away and the question of sexual orientation was examined carefully by Joseph, as prefect, and his team. In July 1992, a document entitled *Some Considerations Concerning the Response to Legislative Proposals on Nondiscrimination of Homosexual Persons* was published. In this document, the prefect argued to legislators that it would not be unjust discrimination to take into account sexual orientation when making laws regarding adoption or foster care, in the employment of teachers or athletic coaches, and in military recruitment. In response to the furor this caused, the prefect replied that "these were real considerations which required in depth study and could not be so easily dismissed." The document decisively condemned any form of harassment or discrimination; it did describe homosexuality as a moral disorder. The debate and the questions surrounding sexuality intensified over the next decade.[6]

These cases represent just a few of the issues that Joseph as the Prefect of the Congregation for the Doctrine of the Faith dealt with.

Cardinal Joseph Ratzinger, center, former archbishop of Munich and Freising and Prefect of the Congregation for the Doctrine of the Faith, speaks at a press conference at the Vatican on October 22, 1984. The main topic of the conference was "Liberation Theology." (AP Photo/Gianni Foggia)

Other significant issues were the Church's understanding of itself as a "communion," the various questions raised by Catholic involvement in politics, and the many anticipated urgent questions that might be raised by biotechnology in the 21st century. After the crisis of sexual abuse and Church leadership failures in the United States came to light, the CDF's role as the Church's court for determining whether men should be removed from the ministry expanded, as did the role of the prefect in reviewing individual cases. Along with all his work as prefect, it was also Joseph's role to support the pope's efforts in interpreting what the Second Vatican Council imposed. He also played a role in the Extraordinary Synod of Bishops summoned by John Paul in 1985 to mark the 20th anniversary of the Council's conclusions and to reflect on what the Council had and had not accomplished. Just prior to the Synod meeting, the book *The Ratzinger Report: An Exclusive Interview on the State of the Church*, published in several languages, was a conversation with the Italian journalist Vittorio Messori. It created a firestorm within the Catholic Church and community, with Cardinal Godfried Danneels of Belgium saying in response to the book in his press conference during the Synod of 1985, "this is not a synod about a book, it's a synod about the Council!" For many, the book itself set the context of the Synod meeting, or at least its agenda. In the book, Joseph noted he was concerned about the misunderstandings of the Council and the effects of those misunderstandings on Catholic theology and Catholic practice.[7]

The Extraordinary Synod of 1985 did not end the divisions in the Church that had been a hallmark of the post-Vatican II period, nor did it solve the problem of rigidity and complicity of the Church. Joseph's role in the Synod of 1985 did not end when the meeting ended, either. One of the recommendations of the meeting was that the Holy See prepare a new universal catechism for the Church. The oversight of this massive, difficult, and time-consuming project fell to Cardinal Ratzinger as chairman of a commission of 12 cardinals and bishops. After nine drafts, the *Catechism of the Catholic Church* was declared official by Pope John Paul II, with the apostolic constitution *Fidei Depositum* (The Deposit of Faith), which was signed by the pope on October 11, 1992, the 30th anniversary of the opening of the Second Vatican Council.[8]

Joseph admitted that his prefecture of the Congregation for the Doctrine of the Faith was one of the most difficult tasks he had undertaken in his service to the Church. The messages regarding difficult issues were often distorted; however, he always maintained his integrity and remained faithful to his episcopal motto, which was to be a coworker for the truth. From the point of view of progressive Catholics, including feminist theologians, and also many American Catholics, Joseph's near-quarter century as Prefect of the Congregation set the Church on a reverse course, to its pre-Vatican II era of conformity and pessimism. To many Catholics, Joseph will always be known as the "Panzer Cardinal" and they describe him as being narrow-minded.[9]

When Joseph was elected pope in 2005, he appointed William Levada, Archbishop of San Francisco, as the new prefect. Levada had previously worked with the Congregation between 1976 and 1982. With this appointment, the new pope and his prefect began a reorganization of the Roman curia.

NOTES

1. George Weigel, *God's Choice: Pope Benedict XVI and the Future of the Catholic Church* (New York: HarperCollins, 2005), 180.

2. Stephen Mansfield, *Pope Benedict XVI: His Life and Mission* (New York: Jeremy P. Tarcher/Penguin, 2005), 7, 8.

3. Weigel, *God's Choice: Pope Benedict XVI and the Future of the Catholic Church*, 180.

4. Ibid., 183.

5. Ibid., 187–189.

6. Michael Collins, *Pope Benedict XVI The First Five Years* (Dublin, Ireland: The Columba Press, 2010), 73–75.

7. Weigel, *God's Choice: Pope Benedict XVI and the Future of the Catholic Church*, 196–197.

8. Ibid., 199–201.

9. Greg Tobin, *Holy Father, Pope Benedict XVI* (New York: Sterling Publishing, 2005), 108.

Chapter 7

THE ASCENDANCE OF
POPE BENEDICT XVI

Because few outside the Vatican knew little about the man just elected as the new pope, the world quickly wanted to know the story of the quiet German scholar who was now the 265th leader of the Roman Catholic Church. While there were messages sent from the Vatican, most of the official announcements provided little background or perspective about Benedict XVI's life or what he intended for the Church. For example, one announcement noted only that Benedict XVI had requested a piano be moved into the papal apartment. Two weeks after the papal election, an official biography was posted on the Vatican's own website; however, it was found to be less than helpful to those wanting, even demanding, information. Vatican insiders touted Benedict XVI's work ethic, saying he would write for 12 hours without eating and dictate 20 pages or more to his secretary at one sitting. Other stories began to circulate; some were true, others were embellished, and still others were quite untrue, bordering on the absurd. Reporters described how Benedict XVI struggled with modern technology and was intimidated by computers. They noted that he had never driven a car and that some of his personal interests were his love of cats, playing the piano, and his enjoyment of Bavarian beer.

To many, especially his students and those he mentored during his long academic career, Benedict XVI was a hero in his devotion to the gospel and Church dogma. In regard to other aspects of the pope's life, there was some apprehension. For example, the man who, many years before, was a part of the Hitler Youth was a concern. Besides, some found it difficult to support him in his new role after he had served as the Vatican's disciplinarian, aggressively leading the Congregation for the Doctrine of Faith against dissent within the Catholic ranks. Long-time colleagues noted the power of Benedict XVI's intellect, saying he could tell jokes in Latin and was a theological encyclopedia. They also rejected his image as a ruthless oppressor and said he was always personal in his dealings; to them, Benedict XVI was firm in his principles and always listened to everyone.

Most of what was initially learned about Pope Benedict XVI came from his own sermons and public statements. It was known that it was his intent to lengthen John Paul II's legacy. It was known that he would fight against abortion; he would hold the line against homosexuality in the Church, prevent the ordination of female priests, and firmly handle the scandalous behavior among priests that had marked the Church in previous years. It was also made known that he intended to fast-track the path to sainthood for John Paul II, something millions around the world viewed positively. As Vatican reporter John Allen wrote in his article in April 2005, Benedict XVI was soon viewed as "tough enough to make difficult political choices, yet profound enough to grasp the deeper theological currents running beneath the political terrain." He was also seen as a man "with a keen vision" and was "aware of the realities facing the Catholic Church."[1] Benedict XVI was also described as having great spiritual depth. When he celebrated mass, his reverence was transparent and few could ever dispute the nobility of his spiritual purpose.

Benedict XVI's personal side was not particularly known to the general public and some held the view that he was cold and detached in his demeanor. To Vatican insiders, however, he was viewed as humble, gentle, gracious, and in some situations, even shy. They said he would be a pope who would inspire his flock and also noted that he could provoke those within the Vatican walls, within the Church itself, and the Church around the world. Evidenced by the speed with which he was elected, the conclave afforded him strong support; certainly, electing a pope on the fourth ballot noted strong consensus among the cardinals, giving Benedict XVI clear authorization to lead the Church according to its history, within its foundations and meanings, and through its problems and challenges. To the conservative side of the Church, Benedict XVI "had the toughness to express the traditional truths of the faith in time of dissent and doubt." To Catholics with a more liberal bent, he was something akin to a "formidable opponent of the many reforms which they have long espoused."[2] Everyone expected Benedict XVI to lead as his mentor and great friend John Paul II had, but they also expected him to lead in his own particular way.

There were those that suspected Benedict XVI would be an interim pope, a continuance, or a transitional pope, especially considering he was 78 when elected. However, Benedict XVI was very aware of the enormous challenges facing the Church. Amid all the speculation of where he would take the Church, one thing soon became certain—Benedict's reign would not be known as a transitional papacy; he would make his own mark on his beloved Catholic Church, always consistent with the faith by which he has lived his whole life. Benedict XVI clearly had specific goals—large and small—that he intended to achieve during his pontificate.

Whatever Catholics and non-Catholics believe about Benedict XVI's views on issues that affect the Church and the world today, he is the leader, the supreme pontiff of the Catholic Church, the oldest and largest religious organization in the world. Before being elected pope, he was appointed by Pope John Paul II to be the head of the Congregation for the Doctrine of the Faith. Before that, he was bishop and a professional theologian. He came to his throne as an intellectual, an academic dedicated to interpreting Church doctrine, theology, and faith. For many years, Benedict XVI wrote on an array of questions affecting his Church and religious life. He has a tranquil confidence in explicit faith and the application of Catholic dogma; thin regard to homosexuality, abortion, and women ordained as priests, there is no shift in the strictness of his beliefs. When Benedict XVI takes on an issue, he begins with what is basic, which to him are the words of Jesus in the gospels. When considering or ruling on an issue, he never misses an opportunity to assert the scripture or Church doctrine, which is often difficult for many to digest, and sometimes to agree with. Still, Benedict XVI is the pope, the enforcer of the faith, and the Catholic world looks to him for direction, for reassurance, and to direct the Church and the issues it faces, according to faith, doctrine, and Catholic dogma.

POPE BENEDICT, SOCIAL ISSUES, AND CATHOLIC CHURCH DOCTRINE
Sexual Abuses within the Catholic Church

A story appeared in *The Boston Globe* on January 6, 2002, about Cardinal Bernard Law's inaction regarding accusations of sexual abuse against a former Boston priest. The story began with what would become the deepest crisis in the history of the Catholic Church in the United States. The reports that Catholic bishops had been aware of charges of sexual abuses against priests and left them in their ministries, or in some cases, transferring them to new assignments without notifying anyone about their pasts, generated extensive anger within the Church, and certainly in the media. Initially, Vatican officials were skeptical about the scandal and the motives behind the allegations. Their statements early on were met with the impression that the Vatican was in denial about how serious the problems were and how widespread the scandals were. One of the officials behind such statements was Cardinal Prefect Joseph Ratzinger. When asked in November 2002 about the media's attention to the scandals associated with the abuse by priests, the response was that "priests were also sinners" and that he was not convinced that "the constant presence in the press of the sins of Catholic priests, especially in the United States, is a planned campaign, as the percentage of these offences among priests is not higher than in other categories, and perhaps even lower." He added, "In the U.S. there was constant news on the alleged abuses and that the attention did not correspond to the objectivity of the information or the objectivity of the facts," and said, "one comes to the conclusion that it is intentional, manipulated, that there is a desire to discredit the Church."[3]

Many felt at the time that the Vatican's responses to the scandals in the United States were evasive. They also felt that officials were trying to minimize the effects of the scandal and blame the media for sensationalizing them. The effects of the abuses and the initial uproar over them within the Church and throughout the country were that the Vatican either did not want to address them or that they were hoping that, at some point, the stories would fade and their aftermath would not have to be addressed. However, as a cardinal and as prefect of the Congregation for the Doctrine of Faith, Ratzinger's office had been given the responsibility of reviewing the accusations, and he soon became aware of the gravity of the situation and the need for the Vatican to respond. As a result of his office's responsibilities early on, as pope, Benedict XVI was well aware of the abuse scandal in the United States. By the fall of 2004, the Congregation, under Ratzinger's leadership, had dealt with more than 500 cases; most of these cases were referred back to the local bishops, authorizing them to take immediate action against the accused priest.[4]

When he became pope, Benedict XVI had had direct experience with the sexual abuse crisis. As pope, he believed in dealing with the accusations directly because he had been a priest himself and had seen reputations tarnished; and because these abuses involved children, he believed them to be profoundly shocking and horrifying. As a result, there was a sense that Pope Benedict XVI was paying attention and that it was his intent to deal with the situations as quickly as possible. To many, his quick response made him "a large part of the solution for the Church and far more than Pope John Paul II, Benedict has been open about the scope of the abuses and the harm inflicted; he has met with abuse victims to express his own personal sorrow, has condemned bishops for their actions—and failures to act—as well the criminal priests they ignored or sheltered; and he has made it clear that it is the welfare of children, not the reputation of the Church, that matters."[5]

"Catholic laity have responded to his efforts and have realized that the cover-ups in many of the cases indicate that steps taken by the Vatican, including when Benedict was Cardinal Ratzinger and the church's disciplinarian in his post as Prefect of the Congregation for the Doctrine of Faith, have been positive."[6] While abuses continue to come to light, they are dealt with as expeditiously as possible, although sometimes not as quickly or as suitably as those involved would like.

While the sexual abuses took place in the United States, there were also scandals in Ireland. In March 2012, the Vatican noted that the Church in Ireland had seen progress in addressing abuses scandals and in reporting new abuse cases directly to Rome; the report also noted that

Past Archbishop Sean Brady of Armagh, Ireland, at left, talks with Pope Benedict XVI after receiving the red three-cornered Cardinal's biretta hat during a consistory inside Saint Peter's Basilica at the Vatican. Benedict XVI met with senior Irish clergy in December of 2009 to discuss a possible response to devastating reports of the Church shielding child-molesting priests. (AP Photo/ Pier Paolo Cito, Pool, File)

would-be priests needed better screening and training, according to the summary of a near year-long investigation by the Vatican. The investigation, an Apostolic Visitation, was announced by Pope Benedict in March 2010, with four high-ranking prelates, abbots, bishops, or cardinals chosen by the pope, conducting the investigation.[7]

The investigation was part of the Vatican's response to the reports by the Irish government that found cases of sexual abuse by priests and also evidence of a wide cover-up of the scandals. At a press conference in Dublin in March 2012, the highest-ranking Catholic official in Ireland, Cardinal Sean Brady, "welcomed the findings and repeated the church's plea for forgiveness from victims." He said, "Innocent young people were abused by clerics and religious to whose care they had been entrusted, while those who should have exercised vigilance often failed to do so effectively."[8] The Irish charity known as "One in Four," which represents child abuse victims, said "it appreciated the summary of the inquiry but that the Vatican still did not accept responsibility for its role in creating the culture that facilitated the cover-ups." The executive director of the charity noted that there had been a "hardening of attitudes" when it came to compensating victims.[9] The scandals led to a crisis within the Irish Church and in Irish society. The summary of the investigation noted that seminaries in Ireland should have stricter admission guidelines and should more effectively train seminarians on matters of child protection, and also stated that greater pastoral attention should be given to victims of sexual abuse and their families.[10]

In June 2012, an international conference celebrating Catholicism—called a eucharistic congress—was held in Ireland. The conference was held despite the country's Catholics' continued anger over child abuses and cover-ups. According to an article in *The Denver Post* on June 11, 2012, an estimated crowd of 12,000 Catholics, many attending from outside Ireland, gathered for a mass held at the start of the week-long conference organized by the Vatican and held every four years in a different part of the world. The last conference, held in Canada in 2008, had the topic of transubstantiation, or the belief that bread and wine transforms during mass into the actual body and blood of Jesus Christ.[11] During the conference in Ireland, an opinion poll was taken of Irish Catholics and it was found that "two-thirds don't believe in transubstantiation, nor do they attend Mass on a weekly basis." The survey was published in *The Irish Times*, and it also found "that 38 percent believe Ireland today would be in worse shape without its dominant church and that three-fifths knew about the Eucharistic Conference that was to be held in Ireland (the survey had a margin of error of 3 percentage points)."[12] These views "noted the rapid secularization, or the removal of the religious elements from everyday life, and the alienation within the church in Ireland."[13] When the conference was last held in Ireland in 1932, more than one million people, or a quarter of the country's population, attended the mass. In 2012, there were protests outside the arena where the mass was held by those that had demanded that Church leaders in Ireland and in Rome admit the child abuses and their protection of pedophile priests; other groups also protested the Church's opposition to homosexuality and the Church's role in most Irish elementary schools and hospitals today.[14]

In America, Catholic bishops gathered in Atlanta, Georgia, in June 2012, for their annual spring meeting. One of the top agenda items at the meeting was assessing the reforms that been adopted 10 years before.

At the meeting in 2002, the bishops approved the Charter for the Protection of Children and Young People, also called the "Dallas Charter." The bishops "vowed in their Charter to put an end to the abuse and the secrecy" surrounding such abuses and "the bishops also pledged to help raise awareness about child abuses in society."[15] In 2012, 10 years after the charter was adopted, "there was not any means of disciplining bishops who failed to follow the charter; it was also noted that each bishop answers to the pope and that Pope Benedict had yet to penalize any of the bishops involved in abuses."[16]

In the 10 years after the charter was adopted in the United States, bishops had taken steps in dealing with child abuses; but in other countries, the Vatican and Church leaders had been not pushed for steps to stop abuses. According to an article by David Gibson, reporting for Religion News Service in an article that appeared in *The Huffington Post Online* in June 2012, "In the U.S., there had been strides in educating Catholics about child sexual abuses and ensuring that children remained safe within Catholic environments. Over the past ten years, Catholic parishes have trained more than 2.1 million clergy, employees, and volunteers about how to create safe environments and in preventing child sexual abuses. Also, more than 5.2 million children have been taught to protect themselves, and churches have run criminal background checks on more than 2 million volunteers, employees, educators, clerics, and seminarians. Such steps have provided for the number of new abuses allegations to decline."[17]

Certainly, when it comes to sexual abuse scandals, there have been dark clouds hovering over the Church, the Vatican, and the pope himself. In responding to the questions of how great the crisis is and if it is one of the greatest in the history of the Church, in a conversation with author and journalist Peter Seewald, Pope Benedict XVI responded that it is a great crisis and upsetting for everyone. He said, "Suddenly so much filth. It was really almost like the crater of a volcano, out of which suddenly a tremendous cloud of filth came, darkening and soiling everything, so that above all the priesthood suddenly seemed to be a place of shame and every priest was under the suspicion of being like that too. Many priests declared that they no longer dared to extend a hand to a child, much less go to a summer camp with children." He said that "the affair was not entirely unexpected and that as prefect [he] had dealt with the cases in the United States and the cases that emerged in Ireland." He added, "But on this scale it was nevertheless an unprecedented shock. . . . I had already met several times with victims of sexual abuse. . . . In October 2006, in my address to the Bishops of Ireland, I had called for them to bring the truth to light, to take whatever steps necessary to prevent such egregious crimes from occurring again, to ensure that the principles of law and justice are fully respected and, above all, to bring healing to the victims. Suddenly to see the priesthood so defiled, and with it the Catholic Church itself, at the very heart—that was something that we were really just beginning to cope with. But it was imperative not to lose sight of the fact that there is good in the Church not only those horrible things." When asked that in light of the burdens on Benedict XVI's papacy caused by the abuse scandals, if he ever considered resigning, Benedict XVI replied, "When the danger is great, one must not run away," and that it was not the time to resign, that he must stand fast and endure a difficult situation. He felt that in a peaceful time, or when a person cannot go on, that may be a time to leave; however, one must not run from danger. When asked if he could ever envision a time for a pope to resign, he replied that when a pope clearly realizes he is no longer capable of handling the duties of his office, then he has the right, and under some circumstances, an obligation to leave.[18]

The Church and Evangelism—The Spreading of Christianity and Ecumenism—Promoting Unity between Different Churches and Groups

The beginning of Pope Benedict XVI's papacy was the time for a new day of Catholic evangelism. At an ordination for 21 new priests, Pope Benedict XVI said that the Church's mission to the world "must continuously put us into motion, make us restless, to bring to those who suffer, to those who are in doubt, and even to those who are reluctant, the joy of Christ."[19] In Benedict XVI's papacy, evangelization would be defined less by mass events, and more by how the Church itself would inspire passions for living according to Catholic beliefs and how to live as an authentic, faithful Christian. Besides, Catholic ministry would be defined by pastoral activities, including celebrations of the sacraments and the actual preaching of the gospel, and less by programs and services that secular, rather than religious, agencies offer. With regard to ecumenism, defined as the unity between different Christian churches and groups, there would be less creation and expansion of structural dimensions of the Catholic Church, and more immersion into the spiritual, liturgical, and ministerial activities connected to and associated with the Catholic Church, with the intention of a strong evident relationship between pastors and worshipers.

Pope Benedict XVI, from the beginning, has had a vision—one that is distinct and clear in Catholic identity and purpose. His intent has been in how faith is spread and understood, and while his vision for the Church in relation to ecumenism and evangelism may seem smaller and less powerful than that of his predecessor, for Benedict XVI, the Church had to be more energetic, a refrain he has insisted on, time and again, and it was vital that the Catholic Church is relevant and its beliefs and Church dogma be understood and followed. Pope Benedict XVI committed himself and the Church to Christian unity since his first message as the newly elected pope. He is committed to ecumenism and having dialogue with other churches, such as the Eastern Orthodox Church, and with churches in the west, including the Lutheranism, Evangelical Christians, and Anglicanism and other Protestant denominations, striving to deepen theological dialogues with these religious bodies and seeking common causes on social and cultural issues.

Pope Benedict XVI called for the Year of Faith, from October 11, 2012, to November 24, 2013, as "a summons to an authentic and renewed conversion to the Lord, the one Savior of the world." Benedict XVI wrote in his apostolic letter *Porta Fidei* (Door of Faith) that, during the year, "we will have the opportunity to profess our faith in the risen Lord in our cathedrals and in the churches of the whole world, in our homes and among our families, so that everyone may feel a strong need to know better and to transmit the future generations the faith of all times." The celebration also commemorated the 50th anniversary of the opening of the Second Vatican Council and the 20th anniversary of the Catechism of the Catholic Church; the year began while Church leaders from around the world gathered in October 2012 for the Synod of Bishops on the New Evangelization.[20]

Benedict XVI opened the first working session of the Synod of Bishops on October 9, 2012, by issuing a call for "renewed evangelical dynamism" in the Church. In his address, he explained how the Church is missionary and that there are two branches of its mission, "the announcement of the Gospel to those who do not yet know Jesus Christ and his message of salvation and . . . the New Evangelization, (which is) directed principally at those who, though baptized, have drifted away from the Church and live without reference to the Christian life."[21]

In his book *The Virtues*, Pope Benedict XVI includes an excerpt from his message of April 13, 2008, about cooperating in evangelization—"The gift of faith calls all Christians to cooperate in the work of evangelization. This awareness must be nourished by preaching and catechesis, by the liturgy, and by constant formation in prayer. It must grow through the practice of welcoming others, with charity and spiritual companionship, through reflections and discernment, as well as pastoral planning, of which attention to vocations must be an integral part."[22]

The Church and Marriage

In the Roman Catholic Church, marriage forms the foundation of the family and the primary purpose of marriage is for procreation and the education of children. In the Church, fertility and procreation are viewed as a gift and are the ultimate goal and purpose of marriage. In his book *The Virtues*, Benedict XVI included the "Marriage as Instrument of Salvation" from his General Address of May 5, 2010, where he said, "God's gift to us of marriage and family life enables us to experience something of the infinite love that unites the three divine persons: Father, Son, and Holy Spirit. Human beings, made in the image and likeness of God, are made for love; indeed at the core of our being, we long to love and to be loved in return. Marriage is truly an instrument of salvation, not only for married people but for the whole of society . . . it places demands upon us, it challenges us, it calls us to be prepared to sacrifice our own interests for the good of the other. It requires us to exercise tolerance and to offer forgiveness. It invites us to nurture and protect the gift of new life."[23]

The Church and Birth Control

Benedict XVI is known to embrace a Benedictine motto, *Succisa virescit*, or "pruned, it grows again." He has raised the prospect of shrinking the

Church to include its true believers and rejecting those who call themselves Catholic without accepting the obligations of faith; this includes accepting the Church's stand on birth control, procreation, and abortion.

In the United States, birth control is morally acceptable to Catholics and to most Americans. Also, in the United States, "89 percent of all Americans and 82 percent of Catholics believe birth control is morally acceptable."[24] In 2012, President Obama and his administration and Catholics in the United States found themselves in a heated discussion about whether employers should be required to offer birth control to their employees. According to a *Wall Street Journal* article, "Americans overwhelmingly agree that employers should be required to offer birth control to their employees; however a slight majority opposed the rule mandating Roman Catholics and other religious institutions from having to provide the service."[25] The 2010 Affordable Care Act, passed by Congress and signed by President Obama, included a mandate that Roman Catholic and other religiously affiliated hospitals and colleges offer birth control paid for by the institutions' insurance companies. In February 2012, President Obama and his administration proposed an accommodation, which some felt provided for a way around the contraception coverage requirement in the healthcare law and addressed the concerns of religious groups over the mandate. In late May 2012, 43 different Catholic groups and institutions, including the University of Notre Dame, the Archdioceses of Washington, New York, and Michigan, and the Catholic University of America, sued the government for the requirement of the 2010 Affordable Care Act on the grounds that it is an overreach of government into the affairs of the Church.[26] The White House issued a statement soon after the lawsuits were announced that asserted it did not want a legal fight with religious groups and that dialogue with Catholic leaders would continue. For many within the Church, including U.S. Catholic bishops, the issue of a mandate to provide birth control benefits was also a First Amendment–religious freedom issue. While public opposition mounted against the mandate, Catholic leaders were charged with the notion they were mounting their opposition and playing politics in a way to assist the Republican Party, especially in a presidential election year.

On May 17, 2012, during his installation ceremony in Baltimore, Archbishop William Lori "defended the cause of religious freedom as a defining issue for the American people and the Catholic faithful," saying, "We do not seek to defend religious liberty for partisan purposes, as some have suggested; we do this because we are lovers of a human dignity that was fashioned and imparted not by the government, but by the Creator." Lori's installation took place one day after the general counsel for the U.S. Conference of Catholic Bishops issued a formal response that "rejected President Obama's and his administration's proposed 'accommodation' to the Health and Human Services mandate" within the healthcare law. Pope Benedict XVI, when U.S. Bishops were visiting the Vatican, "underscored the global significance of the First Amendment fight in the U.S.," saying, "With her long tradition of respect for the right relationship between faith and reason, the Church has a critical role to play in countering cultural currents, which . . . seek to promote notions of freedom detached from moral truth . . . legitimate separation of church and state cannot be taken to mean that the Church must be silent on certain issues, nor that the state may choose not to engage or be engaged by the voices of committed believers in determining the values which will shape the future of the nation."[27]

On June 28, 2012, the Supreme Court of the United States upheld the Affordable Care Act of 2010, including the individual mandate—the requirement that most Americans buy health insurance or pay a fine. The ruling pleased many, including advocates for universal health care and dismayed others; it also set the stage for the fight relating to the right to religious freedom to be held in federal court, with advocates stating that the ruling did not address the issue of requiring religious institutions and individuals to provide co-pay-free abortion drugs and other services. It was also the hope of the Catholic Church that the court's decision would stop the implementation of the Health and Human Services mandate that required employee health plans to provide coverage for what they believe are morally objectionable services. Catholic leaders vowed to continue the First Amendment fight, strengthened by a federal law that they believe threatens the free exercise of religion.

Pope Benedict XVI, in the book *Benedict XVI, Light of the World,* was asked whether the Catholic Church "refuse(s) any regulation of conception whatsoever?" His response was, "No. After all, everyone knows that the church affirms natural regulation of conception, which is not just a method, but also a way of life." When asked if the contraceptive pill is another problem in its own right, he responded, "Yes . . . that if we separate sexuality and fecundity from each other in principle, which is what the use of the pill does, then sexuality becomes arbitrary. Logically, every form of sexuality is of equal value. This approach to fecundity as something apart from sexuality, so far apart that we may even try to produce children rationally and no longer see them as a natural gift, was, after all, quickly followed by the ascription of equal value to homosexuality. . . . Finding ways to enable people to live the teaching, on the other hand, is a further question. . . . We are sinners. But we should not take the failure to live up to this high moral standard as an authoritative objection to the truth. We should try to do as much good as we can and to support and put up each other."[28]

The Church and Celibacy, Homosexuality, and Gay Marriage

In the Roman Catholic Church, the practice of priestly celibacy is theologically based, meaning the Church imitates the life of Jesus in regard to chastity and the sacrifice of married life, and follows the example of Jesus as being "married" to the church. In the Catholic Church, deacons of the Church may be married men; however, they may not be ordained as priests or bishops. The Second Vatican Council allowed for exceptions in that married Protestant priests or ministers who convert to Catholicism and wish to become priests in the Catholic Church may do so as long as their wives consent.

In the past, all that mattered for a priest in regard to sexual orientation was celibacy. If a priest kept his vows, it supposedly did not matter if he were refusing to have sex with a man or a woman. What mattered was that he kept his vows and had sex with no one. Vatican documents in 1975 and 1986 reveal that the Vatican did not support gay sexual intimacy, but recognized homosexuality as "innate" and not, in itself, a sin. Gay people, according to the Vatican, were "often generous and giving of themselves," and the notion that gays could not lead celibate lives was an "unfounded and demeaning assumption." However, the rules changed as of 2005. The Vatican and Pope Benedict XVI ruled that gay priests are barred from serving and cannot be priests. The rules suggest gay sexual orientation threatens "priestly life," and so homosexuals, even if they are celibate, are barred from the priesthood.[29]

The Roman Catholic Church teaches that while homosexual tendencies are not sinful, homosexual acts are, and children should grow up in a traditional family with a mother and a father. In March 2012, Benedict XVI denounced the "powerful political and cultural currents" seeking to legalize gay marriage in the United States. His comments in opposition to homosexual marriage were a part of his address to bishops from the United States on their visit to the Vatican. He said, "Sexual differences cannot be dismissed as irrelevant to the definition of marriage," adding, "the traditional family and marriage had to be defended from every possible misrepresentation of their true nature because whatever injured families injured society." Benedict XVI then said, "In this regard, particular mention must be made of the powerful political and cultural currents seeking to alter the legal definition of marriage (in the United States)." As of January 2013, nine states and the District of Columbia have legalized gay marriage.[30] Benedict XVI, in his March 2012 comments, called on American bishops to continue their "defence (sic) of marriage as a natural institution consisting of a specific communion of persons, essentially rooted in the complementarity (sic) of the sexes and oriented to procreation." Another leading opponent and voice against gay marriage in the United States is New York's Archbishop Timothy Dolan, who was elevated to the rank of cardinal in February 2012. Dolan has fought against gay marriage before it became legal in New York State in June 2011, and in September 2011, he sent a letter to President Obama criticizing the administration's decision not to support a federal ban on gay marriage. He said in the letter that "such a policy could," in his words as president of the U.S. Bishops' Conference, "precipitate a national conflict between Church and state of enormous proportions." The Vatican and Catholic officials around the world have protested against moves to legalize gay marriage in Europe and other developed parts of the world. Gay marriage is legal in a number of European countries, including Spain and the Netherlands.[31]

In March 2012, Benedict XVI urged visiting American bishops to increase their level of teaching about "the evils of premarital sex and cohabitation," and denounced what he called the "powerful gay marriage lobby in America." He added that there was "an urgent need for American Catholics to discover the value of chastity, an essential element of Christian teaching that he said had been subject to unjust 'ridicule.'" He told the visiting bishops not to "back down in the face of 'powerful political and cultural currents seeking to alter the legal definition of marriage.'"[32]

The Vatican released a statement on June 25, 2012, about the abuse scandals—"the sexual abuse scandal has tarnished the image of the priest and contributed to a crisis of priestly vocation in the Roman Catholic Church, while also faulting a widespread 'secularized mentality' and parents' ambition for their children, which leaves 'little space to the possibility of a call to a special vocation.'"[33] The document Pastoral Guidelines for Fostering Vocations to Priestly Ministry, prepared over the seven years by the Vatican's Congregation for Catholic Education says, "candidates to the priesthood shouldn't be accepted if they show signs of being profoundly fragile personalities," and also says, "future priests should learn the importance of their future commitments, in particular with regard to celibacy."[34] The guidelines "acknowledge the choice of celibacy is questioned and adds that erroneous opinions within the church are responsible for a lack of appreciation for those who make the choice to remain celibate."[35] Data presented to the Congregation's undersecretary, the Reverend Angelo Vincenzo Zani, show that priestly vocations over the last 10 years have fallen sharply in Europe, remained stable in North and South America, and have risen significantly in Asia and Africa, "though not enough to offset the rapid growth of Catholics' numbers worldwide."[36]

The Church and Women, Radical Feminism, Catholic Nuns, and the Ordination of Women as Priests

In 1979, when Pope John Paul II arrived in the United States, the president of the nation's most powerful organization of nuns met him with a challenge. In her welcoming address, Sister Theresa Kane called on the pope to include women "in all ministries of our church including the priesthood. The pope was silent."[37] While Kane's call for more inclusion within the Church did not change Vatican policy, it did reveal the growing tensions between the Vatican and American nuns. Over the next decades, tensions continued to mount. In 1988, Harvard University divinity professor Harvey Cox arranged a meeting with Cardinal Joseph Ratzinger, who, at the time, was the Prefect of the Vatican's

Congregation for the Doctrine of the Faith. Before his meeting, he had dinner with a group of Dominican nuns staying in Rome on a retreat. They asked Professor Cox why he was meeting with the cardinal, saying no one paid the prefect any attention. A few decades later, nuns are more than paying attention.[38]

When Pope Benedict XVI was elected pope, some Catholic women were disheartened. More than ever, women were dreaming of becoming more inclusive within the Church, including those that supported change in the teaching that restricted sacramental priesthood to men and the ordination of women. Those that did not support such ordination often felt that the Church, as it is structured, does not listen to women and acknowledge women's concerns. Many thought Benedict XVI as pope would not support any change in regard to women's roles, considering his past positions within the Church, which would not suggest any changes during his papacy. Benedict XVI had expressed concerns with what he suggested were exaggerated forms of the feminist movement, even within the Roman Catholic Church. He also suggested that what feminism promoted was not the Christianity that he knew and what the Church espoused.

In 2004, the Congregation for the Doctrine of the Faith issued a letter to the bishops of the Church on the subject of the collaboration of men and women in the Church. The letter criticized modern thought that created an opposition between men and women, the role of one emphasized to the disadvantage of the other, leading to confusion. The letter cited radical feminism as the source of the confusion. Upon the issuance of this letter, Catholic feminists were critical, saying there was no understanding about feminism, and that the arguments were out of date in today's world. There were also many women within the Church that supported what was called Christian feminism, which endorsed the struggle for women's freedom in social and political realms without devaluing the traditional roles of women as wives and mothers.

Upon the papal election of Benedict XVI, everyone knew that no pope could satisfy everyone on this subject or on the many issues facing the Church, including that of ordination of women. In his former powerful position as the head of the Congregation for the Doctrine of the Faith, Benedict XVI reaffirmed the Roman Catholic Church's practice of males only for the priesthood.

Throughout history, women have not had an authoritative voice in the life of the Roman Catholic Church; however, this does not mean that women do not speak. Writing in the journal *Dialogue: A Journal of Theology*, in the fall of 2005, Cristina Grenholm, a professor of systematic theology in Sweden, said that the election of Benedict XVI, while certainly a global event, was also one that was "traditional." For Benedict XVI and women in the Church, "the open attitude toward the diversity of the church in a diverse contemporary world is, I fear, now envisioned from the perspective of a norm that defines the true church and the true Christian faith. The norm is to remain untouched." "The norm," she writes, "is heavily male, controlled by men." However, "as there are women of all kinds (within the church), silencing them implies also silencing many other groups; with the election of Benedict, the church showed its intent to guard traditional faith against other influences." She continued, "Women do not have an authoritative voice in the life of the Church and are not being listened to on equal terms with their male counterparts; and when the Church defines feminist voices as wrong, it also has consequences for the legitimacy of feminist theologians within other denominations."[39]

German moral theologian Dietmar Mieth, one of the first lay Catholic theologians appointed to a major theological teaching position, first came to know Benedict XVI in the 1960s when he was Professor Ratzinger and a popular progressive theology professor at the University of Tübingen in Germany. In an interview in *U.S. Catholic*, upon the election of Pope Benedict XVI, Mieth was asked about the progress on equal rights for women. He responded that he has advocated for women's ordination, saying, "The main argument for us was not so much that we should catch up with modern society, but that the arguments against ordaining women are not persuasive. They are not well-founded biblically; they are not well-founded in theological anthropology. And it is very difficult to reconcile them with what the church asks of the world and society in terms of valuing women and equal rights for women." Mieth added, "The hopes for Benedict XVI are connected to his intellectual ability, the great riches of his experiences, and a hope that he might remember his more progressive youth. Yet under Pope John Paul II—and Cardinal Ratzinger specifically reinforced this—it was 'to be definitively held' by all Catholics that the church has 'no authority whatsoever' to ordain women. Even the discussion was forbidden."[40] Yet, discussions do continue, both encouraging and pessimistic, on the role of women within the laity and nuns of the Catholic Church.

In April 2012, the Vatican mandated the reform of the largest leadership body for women religious in the United States. The mandate was approved by Benedict XVI at the conclusion of the doctrinal investigation of the Leadership Conference of Women Religious, often known as LCWR, which was conducted with the backing of the Vatican's Congregation for the Doctrine of the Faith. With an association of more than 1,500 leaders of U.S. congregations of women religious, the LCWR represents more than 80 percent of the 57,000 women religious in America.[41] In 2008, the Vatican initiated two investigations of the state of women's religious life in the United States. The first was a general survey of nearly 400 institutes conducted by the Congregation for Institutes of Consecrated Life and Societies of Apostolic Life. The results of this survey have yet to be announced. The second survey was focused on a doctrinal assessment of the LCWR.[42]

The three principal reasons for the investigation in 2008 were—first, the content of talks given during the annual assemblies of the LCWR; the second related to "policies of corporate dissent" that had been announced in letters issued by "leadership teams" of various congregations associated with the LCRW, including some of the organization's officers; and third reason related to themes of "radical feminism" that were expressed in programs and presentations sponsored by the LCWR. In response to these concerns, the CDF appointed Bishop Leonard Blair of Ohio as its delegate to conduct the assessment, which was conducted in 2009 and 2010. The conclusion of the assessment was that the doctrinal and pastoral situation of the LCWR "was grave and a matter of serious concern." It found that the Holy See should intervene with steps necessary to reform the LCWR.[43]

In April 2012, the Vatican issued a report that declared that the LCWR, which represented most American nuns, was found to be straying from Church doctrine and had adopted "radical feminist" views. Sister Simone Campbell, head of the Catholic Social Justice Lobby Network, said it felt "like a sock in the stomach."[44] Such a reprimand came as a shock to many U.S. nuns; however, observers noted that confrontation had been brewing since the Second Vatican Council of

1962–1965. The Council asked that religious orders modernize, which many American nuns saw as a focus more on social justice and other issues in their communities and less on spreading Church doctrine, including the social issues of birth control and abortion. Jesuit priest and culture editor for *America* magazine, a Catholic weekly, Reverend James Martin, said Vatican II "asked them to respond to the needs of society," and added that "changes (suggested by Vatican II) have largely fallen out of favor in Rome and has left many nuns in the middle." He noted, "They have embraced the reforms of the Second Vatican Council, and they have thrown themselves into work for the poor and marginalized that other parts of the church wouldn't go near." The nuns, Martin says, have still been following the reforms put in place years ago.[45]

The remedies set forth by the Vatican include a five-year period in which Seattle Archbishop Peter Sartain, along with two other bishops, will provide "review (and) guidance and approval, where necessary, of the work of the LCWR," as noted in the CDF doctrinal assessment.[46] Mary E. Hunt, a feminist theologian, writer, and activist, noted that, "It means they'll review all policies, all speakers, all conferences, all publications and all letters of support."[47] The choices for the members of the LCWR include agreeing to work with the Vatican on making the mandated changes or choose to form a new organization that is independent of the Church's hierarchy. A statement by a group spokesperson said, "The conference plans to move slowly, not rushing to judgment. We will engage in dialogue where possible and be open to the movement of the Holy Spirit."[48] Data collected by the Center for Applied Research in the Apostolate revealed that the Vatican's oversight of nuns in the United States might hurt the recruitment of nuns, whose numbers have already shrunk by two-thirds in the years since Vatican II.[49]

NOTES

1. John L. Allen, "Not a Transitional Pope: Benedict May Surprise," *National Catholic Reporter*, April 29, 2005, 5–8.

2. Ibid.

3. John L. Allen, *The Rise of Benedict XVI* (New York: Doubleday, 2005), 221–222.

4. Ibid., 222.

5. Brian Bethune, "Is the Pope Catholic?" *Macleans*, April 18, 2011, www2.macleans.ca/2011/04/18/rebel-with-a-cross.

6. Ibid.

7. Rachel Donadio, "Vatican Inquiry Finds Progress in Irish Abuse Scandal," *New York Times*, March 20, 2012, www.nytimes.com.

8. Ibid.

9. Ibid.

10. Ibid.

11. Shawn Pogatchnik, "Catholics Find Skeptics," *The Denver Post*, June 11, 2012, 12A.

12. Ibid.

13. Ibid.

14. Ibid.

15. David Gibson, "10 Years After Catholic Sex Abuse Reforms, What's Changed?" *Huffington Post Online*, June 7, 2012, http://www.huffingtonpost.com.

16. Ibid.

17. Ibid.

18. Peter Seewald, *Benedict XVI*, *Light of the World* (San Francisco: Ignatius Press, 2010), 23–24, 29–30.

19. Stephen Mansfield, *Pope Benedict XVI: His Life and Mission* (New York: Jeremy P. Tarcher/Penguin, 2005), 149–153.

20. "U.S. Bishops, Apostolates Ring in the Year of Faith," *National Catholic Register*, October 10, 2012, http://www.ncregister.com.

21. "Pope 'Working Harder Than Anyone' at Synod Sessions," *National Catholic Register*, October 10, 2012, http://www.ncregister.com.

22. Pope Benedict XVI, *The Virtues* (Huntington, IN: One Sunday Visitor Publishing Division, Our Sunday Visitor, Inc., 2010), 25.

23. Ibid., 72–73.

24. Samreen Hooda, "Birth Control Morally Acceptable to Catholics, Most Americans," *The Huffington Post Online*, June 7, 2012, http://www.huffingtonpost.com.

25. Ibid.

26. Joan Frawley Desmond, "Bishops Defend Legal Strategy as HHS Mandate Emerges as Election-Year Issue," *National Catholic Register*, May 30, 2012, http://www.ncregister.com.

27. Joan Frawley Desmond, "Installed at Baltimore's Cathedral, Archbishop Lori Draws Line in Sand for Courageous Faith," *National Catholic Register*, May 17, 2012, http://www.ncregister.com.

28. Seewald, *Benedict XVI, Light of the World*, 146,147.

29. Andrew Sullivan, "The Vatican's New Stereotype," *Time*, December 12, 2005, 92.

30. Carole Feldman, "Same-Sex couples can't file joint federal taxes," Associated Press, January 22, 2013, http://news.yahoo.com.

31. Philip Pullella, "Pope Denounces U.S. Efforts to Legalize Gay Marriage," *Huffington Post Online*, March 9, 2012, http://www.huffingtonpost.com.

32. "Vatican: Pope Presses U.S. Bishops on Message on Sex," *Associated Press*, March 10, 2012, http://www.nytimes.com.

33. "Vatican Blames Lack of Priests on Secularism, Abuse, Parents," *Huffington Post*, June 25, 2012, http://www.huffingtonpost.com.

34. Ibid.

35. Ibid.

36. Ibid.

37. Stephanie Simon, "Vatican Crackdown on Nuns Over Social Justice Issues, Women Ordination," *Reuters*, April 20, 2012, http://www.huffingtonpostonline.

38. Scott Newman, "Nuns and the Vatican: A Clash Decades in Making," *NPR*, May 3, 2012, http://www.npr.org.

39. Cristina Grenholm, "A New Pope and Voices That Deviate from the Norm," *Dialog: A Journal of Theology*, Fall 2005, 304–306.

40. "How Will Benedict Rule?" *U.S. Catholic*, June 2005, 30–34.

41. Jimmy Akin, "Holy See Mandates Reform of U.S. Women Religious' Conference," *National Catholic Register*, April 19, 2012, http://www.ncregister.com.

42. Ibid.

43. Ibid.

44. Scott Newman, "Nuns and the Vatican: A Clash Decades in Making," *NPR*, May 3, 2012, http://www.npr.org.

45. Ibid.

46. Ibid.

47. Ibid.

48. Ibid.

49. Ibid.

Chapter 8

THE PERSPECTIVES OF
POPE BENEDICT XVI

"The pope must not proclaim his own ideas, but ever link himself and the Church to obedience to the Word of God, when faced with all attempts of adaptation or of watering down, as with all opportunism."

—*Homily at the Basilica of Saint John in Lateran,*
Rome, May 7, 2005[1]

When elected pope, Benedict XVI was more than likely the first academic theologian in two centuries; early on in his religious life, he chose teaching theology, and with his academic life came intellectual writing. From his first position as parish priest and on to serving as pope, Benedict XVI has continued to write on various topics that affect his Church. However, there have been a few times in his career where he has had to consider how a new opportunity would affect his academic life and his service to the Church. Such was the case when Pope John Paul II asked him to leave his position as Archbishop of Munich and accept the position of Prefect of the Congregation for the Doctrine of the Faith (CDF). Leaving his diocese in Munich was a difficult choice and turning down his friend and the pope was certainly not easy either, and Joseph hesitated. One reason for his pause was that he thought he would have to give up his personal writing projects. As prefect, he knew he would have to spend most of his time on what pertained to proceedings and conflicts as they came to light within the Church. In discussions with the pope, Joseph proposed that he not give up his intellectual work entirely and the pope agreed that he should continue to work on his own theological writing—an important aspect of his religious life.

During his time in service to the Church, and throughout his career as theologian, professor, and as pope, Benedict XVI's personal writing productivity has been extraordinary. When elected pope in 2005, he brought to his papacy more than a half-century of writings that have

Joseph Ratzinger presents a book with the documents issued by the Congregation for the Doctrine of the Faith during a press conference at the Vatican in 1985, before his tenure as pope. The Vatican is enforcing copyright on Pope Benedict XVI's writings and speeches and seeking royalties, for both recent works and those that the theologian penned in the decades before becoming pontiff. (AP Photo/Bruno Mosconi)

included reflections on his faith and what he believes to be the truths about the Bible, Christianity, the Catholic Church, Church liturgy and dogma; what Benedict XVI believes and what he directs his flock to believe, without question, influence contemporary situations and issues.

When Benedict XVI is asked a question or when asked what his perspective is on an issue, before he begins his discussion, he pauses, thinks carefully, and then often in a complete paragraph or two, and often in one of his second, third, or even his seventh language, he answers with his extensive knowledge on almost any subject in a voice that is arguably second to only a few. For instance, in 1996, in his book entitled *Salt of the Earth*, author Peter Seewald interviewed Cardinal Joseph Ratzinger, who at the time was prefect of the CDF. Seewald notes in his foreword that Joseph is "considered, especially in his homeland, a combative but also controversial churchman . . . and few people are more painfully aware of the losses and the drama of the Church than this shrewd man of simple background from rural Bavaria. . . . I asked him how many ways to God there were . . . the Cardinal didn't take long to answer: As many, he said, as there are people."[2] In the book, Seewald posed the question of whether Joseph has "remained true to himself and noted that for many, there are two Ratzingers: the conservative one and stern guardian of the faith in Rome, and the former as a theological progressive." In his answer, Joseph stated that basic decisions of his life are continuous, that he believes in God, in Christ, in the Church, and tries to orient his life accordingly. He added that the ages in life change a man and he should not try to be a 17-year-old when he is 70, or vice versa, "I want to be true to what I have recognized as essential and also to remain open to seeing what should change . . . what surrounds a man also changes his position . . . the circumstances give one's words and actions another value . . . that I, precisely in changing, have tried to remain faithful to what I have always had at heart . . . to live is to change and that the one who was capable of changing has lived much."[3]

Author Seewald asked Joseph about the virtues of faith, hope, charity, and what they mean in the life of the cardinal. Joseph answered that "faith is the root that opens up the basic decision to perceive God, to take God at his word, and to accept him . . . the key that explains everything else." He added, "faith implies hope . . . the world is not simply good, nor should it stay that way . . . to have Christian hope means to know about evil and yet to go to meet the future with confidence . . . hope contains the element of confidence in the face of our imperiled history . . . the expectation of the better world supports no one, for it's not our world, and everyone has to deal with his world, with his future. The world of the coming generations is essentially molded by the freedom of these generations and can be determined by us in advance only to a very limited extent. But eternal life is indeed my future and thus a power that shapes history."[4]

Author Seewald noted that Joseph once wrote, "History is marked by the conflict between love and the inability to love, that desolation of souls that occurs when man is capable of recognizing only the quantifiable values as valuable . . . this destruction of the capacity to love gives birth to deadly boredom. It is the poisoning of man. If it carried the day, man, and with him also the world, would be destroyed." Seewald posed the question of what God really wants from us? Joseph, in his answer, referred to Goethe, who said that "history as a whole is the struggle between belief and unbelief," and noted that Saint Augustine saw this differently, saying, "it is a struggle between two kinds of love, between the love of God unto sacrifice of self, and self-love unto the denial of God . . . depicted history as the drama of a struggle between two kinds of love." Joseph further stated, "History as a whole is the struggle between love and the inability to love, between love and the refusal to love. This is also . . . something we are experiencing again today, when man's independence is pushed to the point where he says: I don't want to love at all, because then I make myself dependent, and that contradicts my freedom . . . love means being dependent on something that perhaps can be taken away from me . . . introduces a huge risk of suffering into my life . . . the express or tacit refusal: Before having constantly to bear this risk, before seeing my self-determination limited, before coming to depend on something I can't control so that I can suddenly plunge into nothingness, I would rather not have love . . . the decision that comes from Christ is another: Yes to love, for it alone, precisely with the risk of suffering and the risk of losing oneself, bring man to himself and makes him what he should be . . . that is really the true drama of history. In the many opposing fronts it can ultimately be reduced to this formula: Yes or no to love." In his response to what God wants from us, he answered,

"That we become loving persons, for then we are his images . . . for he is . . . love itself, and wants there to be creatures who are similar to him . . . out of the freedom of their own loving, become like him and belong in his company and thus . . . spread the radiance that is his."[5]

As with other powerful world leaders, as pope, Benedict XVI's time is tightly scheduled. And as for many world leaders, his daily responsibilities as pope astound those around him, especially considering Benedict XVI's age and chronic health problems. Yet, Benedict XVI continues to write and carry out his countless duties. Besides his own writings, he also issues encyclicals, gives homilies at mass and during holy visits, delivers messages during Lent and events such as World Day of Peace, World Youth Day, and World Mission Day, issues Apostolic letters or declarations and official statements, gives speeches at events and ceremonies, and holds audiences where he meets with and greets visitors, pilgrims, groups, government officials, and dignitaries.

ENCYCLICAL LETTERS

Benedict XVI's first encyclical letter, issued on December 25, 2005, was entitled *Deus Caritas Est* or "God is Love." On that Christmas Day in Saint Peter's Square, the pope said that "being Christian is not the result of an ethical choice or a lofty idea, but the encounter with an event, a person, which gives life a new horizon and a decisive direction. . . . In a world where the name of God is sometimes associated with vengeance or even a duty of hatred and violence, this message is both timely and significant. . . . I wish to speak of the love which God lavishes upon us and which we in turn must share with others. That is what the two main parts of this Letter are about, and they are profoundly interconnected. The first part is more speculative, since I wanted here–at the beginning of my Pontificate—to clarify some essential facts concerning the love which God mysteriously and gratuitously offers to man, together with the intrinsic link between that Love and the reality of human love. The second part is more concrete, since it treats the ecclesial exercise of the commandment of love of neighbor. The argument has vast implications . . . to call forth in the world renewed energy and commitment in the human response to God's love."[6]

Benedict XVI's second encyclical letter was issued on November 30, 2007, on the topic of *Spe Salvi*, "To the Bishops, Priests and Deacons, Men and Women Religious and All the Lay Faithful on Christian Hope." Benedict wrote, *"SPE SALVI facti sumus*, in hope we were saved, and according to the Christian faith, redemption—salvation—is not simply a given. Redemption is offered to us in the sense that we have been given hope, trustworthy hope, by virtue of which we can face our present: the present, even if it is arduous, can be lived and accepted if it leads towards a goal, if we can be sure of this goal, and if this goal is great enough to justify the effort of the journey." He then asks the questions—"what sort of hope could ever justify the statement that, on the basis of that hope and simply because it exists, we are redeemed? And what sort of certainty is involved here?" In his letter, he discusses the topics of "Faith is Hope," and "the concept of faith-based hope," and "faith-hope in the modern age, the shape of Christian hope, learning and practicing hope."[7]

Benedict XVI's third encyclical letter was issued on June 29, 2009, entitled *Caritas in Veritate*, "To the Bishops, Priests and Deacons, Men and Women Religious, the Lay Faithful and All People of Good Will on Integral Human Development in Charity and Truth." Benedict XVI wrote, "Charity in truth . . . is the principal driving force behind the authentic development of every person and all of humanity. Love—*caritas*—is an extraordinary force which leads people to opt for courageous and generous engagement in the field of justice and peace . . . a force that has its origin in God, Eternal Love and Absolute Truth. Each person finds his good by adherence to God's plan for him, in order to realize it fully: in this plan, he finds his truth, and through adherence to this truth he becomes free. To defend the truth, to articulate it with humility and conviction, and to bear witness to it in life are therefore exacting and indispensable forms of charity. . . . All people feel the interior impulse to love authentically: love and truth never abandon them completely. . . . The search for love and truth is purified and liberated by Jesus Christ from the impoverishment that our humanity brings to it. . . . In Christ, *charity in truth* becomes the Face of his Person, a vocation for us to love our brothers and sisters in the truth of his plan."[8]

PASTORAL LETTERS

In March 2010, Benedict XVI issued a pastoral letter to the Catholics of Ireland, entitled "Serious Sins against Defenseless Children." In the letter, he wrote that he shared "in the dismay and the sense of betrayal that so many of you have experienced on learning of these sinful and criminal acts and the way Church authorities in Ireland dealt with them." He wrote of his conviction that "in order to recover, the Church in Ireland must acknowledge the serious sins committed against children" and that "such an acknowledgement, accompanied by sincere sorrow for the damage caused to these victims and their families must lead to a concerted effort to ensure the protection of children from similar crimes in the future." He described what gave rise to the crisis, "a diagnosis of the causes and the effective remedies to be found" and he concluded, "the inadequate procedures for determining the suitability of candidates for the priesthood and religious life, insufficient human, moral, intellectual, and spiritual formation in seminaries and novitiates; tendency in society to favor the clergy and other authority figures, and a misplaced concern for the reputation of the Church and avoidance of scandal, resulting in failure to apply existing canonical penalties and safeguards for the dignity of everyone, were contributing factors." He directly addressed the victims of the abuse and their families, noting his "sorrow and shame and how their trust had been betrayed and dignity violated." He addressed the priests who had abused children and "how they had betrayed the truth that was placed on them . . . urging them to examine their conscience, take responsibility for the sins and openly acknowledge guilt"; and in his address to his bishops, he wrote that "it cannot be denied that they and their predecessors had failed to apply long-established norms of canon law to the crime of child abuse, that serious mistakes were made in responding to the allegations." He recognized how "difficult it was to grasp the extent and complexity of the problem, to obtain information and to make the right decisions in light of conflicting expert advice." He wrote, "Only decisive action carried out with complete honesty and transparency will restore the respect and good will of the Irish people towards the church to which we have consecrated our lives."[9]

HOMILIES AND BOOKS

Just days before his election as pope, Benedict XVI delivered a homily at the funeral mass for John Paul II on April 8, 2005. One of the themes in the sermon was "Follow Me," "the saying of Christ that is also taken as the key to understanding the message that comes to us from the life of our late beloved Pope John Paul II." Benedict XVI noted how John Paul II had "heard the voice of the Lord" while surrounded and threatened by Nazi terrors and how he had studied secretly for the priesthood. He spoke of how John Paul II, in his letters to priests and in his books, interpreted his priesthood with references to the sayings of the Lord, that included "being chosen by God to serve, a shepherd laying down his life for his sheep, and as the Father loves us, so do I also love; these sayings were the heart and soul of John Paul."[10]

In his first homily as Pope Benedict XVI on April 20, 2005, Benedict XVI said that there were two contrasting sentiments—one was "a sense of inadequacy and human turmoil for the responsibility entrusted to me . . . the sense of profound gratitude to God . . . who does not abandon his flock, but leads it throughout time, under the guidance of those whom he has chosen as vicars of his Son, and made pastors."[11] He said he felt the presence of John Paul II and felt his predecessor was telling him to not be afraid. He said, "If the weight of the responsibility that now lies on my poor shoulders is enormous, the divine power on which I can count is surely immeasurable . . . electing me Bishop of Rome, the Lord wanted me as his vicar, he wished me to be the 'rock' upon which everyone may rest with confidence. I ask him . . . that I may be a courageous and faithful pastor of his flock, always docile to the inspirations of his Spirit."[12] He asked for the prayers and collaboration of the cardinals and spoke of the Church today and how it "must revive within herself an awareness of the task to present the world again with the voice of the one who said: 'I am the light of the world: he who follows me will not walk in darkness but will have the light of life.' In undertaking his ministry, the new pope knows that his task is to bring the light of Christ to shine before the men and women of today: not his own light but that of Christ."[13] Benedict XVI noted that he addresses himself to everyone, even those who follow other religious, and addresses "everyone with simplicity and affection, assuring them that the church wants to continue to build an open and sincere dialogue with them, in a search for the true good of mankind and of society."[14] Benedict XVI promised dialogue that John Paul II had begun with various civilizations to "give rise to conditions for a better future for everyone."[15]

In his book *Credo for Today*, Benedict XVI writes an essay entitled "What It Means to Be a Christian, Over Everything: Love." He writes, "Whoever loves is a Christian, and that practicing Christian love in the same way as Christ means that we are good to someone who needs our kindness, even if we do not like him . . . committing ourselves to the way of Jesus Christ. Becoming a Christian . . . is something quite simple and yet completely revolutionary." Answering the question "Why do we need faith?" Benedict writes that "being a Christian means having love . . . That is unbelievably difficult and at the same time, incredibly simple." He writes that "ultimately, faith means nothing other than admitting that we have this kind of shortfall; it means opening our hand and accepting a gift . . . faith is nothing but reaching that point in love at which we recognize that we, too, need to be given something. Faith is thus that stage in love which really distinguishes it as love; it consists in overcoming the complacency and self-satisfaction of the person who says, 'I have done everything, I don't need any further help.' It is only in 'faith' like this that selfishness, the real opposite of love, comes to an end . . . faith is already present in and with true loving; it simply represents that impulse in love which leads to its finding its true self . . . " In the end," Benedict XVI writes, "through talking about love, we came upon faith . . . faith is present within love and that only faith can bring love to its proper end, because our own loving would remain just as inadequate as an open hand stretched out into emptiness."[16]

In this same book *Credo for Today*, Benedict XVI writes an essay entitled "The Church's Credo." In discussing the question of "Why I remain in the Church," he writes,

I remain in the Church because I view the faith—which can be practiced only in her and ultimately not against her—as a necessity for man, indeed, for the world, which lives on that faith even when it does not share it. For if there is no more God—and a silent God is no God—then there is no longer any truth that is accessible to the world and to man. In a world without truth . . . one cannot keep on living; even if we suppose that we can do without truth, we still feed on the quiet hope that it has not yet really disappeared, just as the light of the sun could remain for a while after the sun came to an end, momentarily disguising the worldwide night that had started. . . . I remain in the Church because only the Church's faith saves man. . . . In our world of compulsions and frustrations, the longing for salvation has reawakened with hurricane force. . . . The more liberated, enlightened, and powerful man becomes, the more the longing for salvation gnaws at him, the less free he finds himself. . . . A world free of dominion, suffering, and injustice has become the great slogan of our generation. . . . To fight against suffering and injustice in the world is indeed a thoroughly Christian impulse. But the notion that one can produce a world without suffering through social reform, through the abolition of government and the legal order, and the desire to achieve this here and now are symptoms of false doctrine, of a profound misunderstanding of human nature. Inequality of ownership and power . . . are not the only causes of suffering in this world. And suffering is not just the burden that man should throw off: anyone who tries to do that must flee into the illusory world of drugs so as to destroy himself in earnest and come into conflict with reality. . . . A human being always sees only as much as he loves . . . there is also the clear-sightedness of denial and hatred. But they can see only what is suited to them: the negative. . . . Without a certain measure of love, one finds nothing. . . . One thing ought to be clear: Real love is neither static nor uncritical. If there is any possibility at all of changing another human being for the better, then it is only by loving him and by slowly helping him to change from what he is into what he can be.

Benedict writes, "It is the same within the Church. Staying in a Church that we actually have to make first in order for her to be worth staying in is just not worthwhile; it is self-contradictory. Remaining in the Church because she is worthy of remaining; because she is worth loving and transforming ever anew through love so that she transcends herself and becomes more fully herself–that is the path that the responsibility of faith shows us even today."[17]

In 2010, Benedict XVI wrote his book *The Virtues*, where he discusses theological virtues—faith, hope, and charity, and the cardinal virtues—prudence, justice, fortitude, and temperance. Over the course of his career, Benedict XVI often included these themes in writings and speeches. On faith, he writes that "only sincere dialogue, open to the truth of the Gospel, could guide the Church on her journey. . . . It is a lesson that we too must learn . . . let us all allow ourselves to be guided by the Spirit, seeking to live in the freedom that is guided by faith in Christ and expressed in service to the brethren. It is essential to be conformed ever more closely to Christ. In this way one becomes really free, in this way the Law's deepest core is expressed within us: love for God and neighbor."[18] On the virtue of hope, Benedict XVI follows Saint Thomas Aquinas' last work, the *Compendium Theologiae*, where he "equates hope with prayer." Benedict XVI writes that "prayer is hope in action . . . true reason is contained in prayer, which is why it is possible to hope: we can come into contact with the Lord of the world, he listens to us, and we can listen to him . . . the truly great thing in Christianity, which does not dispense one from small, daily things but must not be concealed by them either, is this ability to come into contact with God."[19]

Benedict XVI also writes about the virtue of charity and how it is the heart of the Christian faith, the centrality of love, and the essential role that charity plays in the pursuit of justice. Charity, he writes, "not only enables justice to become more inventive and to meet new challenges; it also inspires and purifies humanity's efforts to achieve authentic justice and thus the building of a society worthy of man." He continued that "charity is an essential activity and love for widows and orphans, prisoners, and the sick and needy of every kind, is as essential to her as the ministry of the sacraments and preaching of the Gospel. The Church cannot neglect the service of charity any more than she can neglect the Sacraments and the Word."[20]

In part two of his book *The Virtues*, Benedict XVI writes about the cardinal virtues, prudence, justice, fortitude, and temperance. Prudence, Benedict XVI writes, "is the virtue that disposes practical reason to discern our true good in every circumstance and to choose the right means of achieving it; this is not to be confused with timidity or fear, not with duplicity or dissimulation. It guides the other virtues by setting rule and measure and it is prudence that immediately guides the judgment of conscience. The prudent man determines and directs his conduct in accordance with his judgment. With the help of this virtue, we apply moral principles to particular cases without error and overcome doubts about the good to achieve and the evil to avoid."[21]

In regard to the virtue of justice, Benedict XVI writes that it "is the moral virtue that consists in the constant and firm will to give their due to God and neighbor. Justice toward God is called the 'virtue of religion' and justice toward men disposes one to respect the rights of each and to establish in human relationships the harmony that promotes equity with regard to persons and to the common good." On the virtue of fortitude, Benedict XVI writes, it "Is the moral virtue that ensures firmness in difficulties and constancy in the pursuit of the good. It strengthens the resolve to resist temptations and to overcome obstacles in the moral life; fortitude enables one to conquer fear, even fear of death, and to face trials and persecutions and disposes one even to renounce and sacrifice his life in defense of a just cause." The virtue of temperance is, he writes, "The moral virtue that moderates the attraction of pleasures and provides balance in the use of created goods. It ensures the will's mastery over instincts and keeps desires within the limits of what is honorable. A temperate person directs the sensitive appetites toward what is good and maintains a healthy discretion."[22]

As part of his book *The Virtues*, Benedict XVI to writes that "priests are called to be human and the priest must be on God's side." The priest, he writes, "must be man, human in all senses, live true humanity, true humanism; he must be educated, have a human formation, human virtues; develop his intelligence, will, sentiments, affections, and must be a true man according to the will of the Creator." Benedict XVI writes that "human means being generous, being good, and being a just person." He continues, "Education of children with media should be positive and children exposed to what is aesthetically and morally excellent are helped to develop appreciation, prudence, and the skills of discernment." He notes that "it is important to recognize the fundamental value of parents' example and the benefits of introducing young people to classics in literature, to the fine arts, and uplifting music." He writes that "media education requires the exercise of freedom," which he says is "a demanding task." Benedict XVI also addresses suffering, writing that "it is a part of our human existence, stemming from our finitude and from the mass of sin accumulated over the course of history and continues to grow today." He writes that "we must do whatever we can to reduce suffering, and that these are the obligations both in justice and in love, and are among fundamental requirements of the Christian life and human life."[23]

One of Pope Benedict XVI's most widely read and considered by many to be his most important work is *Introduction to Christianity*; it is described as an explanation of the Apostles' Creed and an interpretation of the very foundation of Christianity. Originally published in 1968, it was revised in English, with editions in 1990 and 2004; the latest edition includes a preface by then Joseph Cardinal Ratzinger and prefect of the CDF. The book is dedicated to his university students in Freising, Bonn, Münster, and Tübingen. Covering the many changes and significant events in the Church, the book covers the cardinal's approach to the essential spiritual needs of man. At the center of the book is the question of God and of Christ and that the place of faith is in the Church itself. Written when he was a cardinal, Benedict XVI provides his views on issues and topics stemming from his years as a theologian, on the interpretation of the foundations of Christianity, and the basic truths from his years of study of the Scripture and the history of theology.

The introduction of the book is entitled "I Believe—Amen," with chapters on "The belief in the world of today" and "The ecclesiastical form of faith." Part one, entitled "God" covers the biblical belief in God, the God of faith and of the philosophers, faith in God today, and belief in the Triune God. Part two, entitled "Jesus Christ" covers the problem of faith in Jesus today, the basic form of the "Christological Profession of Faith," the true God and true man, and the different paths taken by Christology (the branch of theology concerned with the study of nature, character, and actions of Jesus Christ), and the development of faith in Christ. Part three, entitled "The Spirit and the Church" covers the unity of the last statements in the creed and the two major questions posed by the articles on the spirit and the Church.

In his preface, Cardinal Ratzinger discusses how world history has moved along at a quick pace and how there were important milestones in the final decades of the millennium. He notes that 1968 was marked by the rebellion of a new generation and that "young people wanted to improve things . . . to bring about freedom, equality and justice, and they were convinced that they had found the way to a better world in the mainstream of Marxist thought." He asks the question—"In such a perplexing situation, should not Christianity try very seriously to rediscover its voice, so as to 'introduce' the new millennium to its message and to make it comprehensible as a general guide for the future?" And he asks, "Where was the voice of the Christian faith at that time?" At the time Joseph wrote the book, he noted that the Second Vatican Council had intended "to endow Christianity once more with the power to shape history . . . that religion belonged to the subjective, private realm and should have its place there . . . following the Council, it was supposed to become evident again that the faith of Christians embraces all of life, that it stands in the midst of history and in time and has relevance beyond the realm of subjective notions. . . . Christianity—at least from the viewpoint of the Catholic Church—was trying to emerge again from the ghetto to which it had been relegated since the nineteenth century and to become involved once more in the world at large."[24]

At the end of Joseph's preface, he notes that if he had to write the book over again, that after all the experiences over more than 30 years, he would have to include "the context of interreligious discussion to a much greater degree than what was appropriate in the initial edition." He believes, however, that "it was appropriate in his fundamental approach that he put the question of God and the question about Christ in the very center, which leads to a 'narrative Christology' and demonstrates that the place of faith is in the church." He adds that, "This basic orientation was correct," and that is why he places the book (in the year 2000), once again, into the hands of his readers.[25]

Prior to becoming pope, Benedict XVI devoted a career to several decades to teaching, writing, and church administration. Over his career, his writing output has been vast—books, essays, documents, sermons, speeches, talks, and interviews; all forms of nonfiction have been produced. Other works written by Benedict XVI as pope and as Cardinal Ratzinger include *God of Jesus Christ* (1978), *Feast of Faith* (1986), *Principles of Christian Morality* (1986), *Principles of Catholic Theology* (1987), *Eschatology* (1989), *In the Beginning . . . A Catholic Understanding of the*

Story of Creation and the Fall (1990, 1995), *To Look on Christ* (1991), *Co-Workers of the Truth* (1992), *The Meaning of Christian Brotherhood* (1993), *A Turning Point for Europe?* (1994), *The Nature and Mission of Theology* (1995), *Salt of the Earth* (1997), *Catechism of the Catholic Church* (1998), *Milestones: Memoirs 1992–1977* (1998), *The Spirit of the Liturgy* (2000), *God and the World* (2002), *God Is Near Us* (2003), *Truth and Tolerance* (2004), *Pilgrim Fellowship of Faith* (2005), *On the Way to Christ* (2005), *Legacy of John Paul II* (2005), *Without Roots* (2006), *Jesus of Nazareth* (2007), *The Apostles* (2007), *Church Fathers* (2008), *Heart of the Christian Life* (2010), and *Doctors of the Church* (2011).

For a great many reasons, there is no disputing the fact that Pope Benedict XVI is one of the greatest intellectuals in the history of the Catholic Church. However, he is known for much more than that. For Pope Benedict XVI, knowledge and intellect are not ends in themselves; their scope is not limited to in-depth studies or learned discourse. To him, the Christian faith is not a kind of knowledge, but rather, it is trust and joy; he believes that someone who is glad from the bottom of his heart, and someone who has suffered and has not lost the capacity for joy, cannot be far from God. In his book *Light of the World*, author Peter Seewald wrote that Benedict XVI is "a teacher to whom any sensible person would want to give a fair hearing. That this teacher is also a pastor, and a thoroughgoing Christian disciple who believes that friendship with Jesus is the key to human happiness." He writes that Benedict XVI is "reforming the papacy by returning it to its evangelical roots as an office of witness to the truth of God in Christ."[26]

For all that he is, all that he has accomplished, and what he has endured over the course of his life; and all that he believes and has given to the Catholic Church, to understand, to know who Benedict XVI is, he may have said it best when, in his inaugural homily at Saint Peter's Square in Rome on April 24, 2005, he said of the papacy— "And now, at this moment, weak servant of God that I am, I must assume this enormous task, which truly exceeds all human capacity."[27]

NOTES

1. Stephen Mansfield, *Pope Benedict XVI: His Life and Mission* (New York: Jeremy P. Tarcher/Penguin, 2005), 165.

2. Cardinal Joseph Ratzinger, *Salt of the Earth: Christianity and the Catholic Church at the End of the Millennium* (San Francisco: Ignatius Press, 2005), 8.

3. Ibid., 115–116.

4. Ibid., 117–118.

5. Ibid., 282–283.

6. Pope Benedict XVI, *Deus Caritas Est,* Encyclical Letter, December 25, 2005, http://www.vatican.va.

7. Ibid.

8. Ibid.

9. Peter Seewald, *Benedict XVI, Light of the World* (San Francisco: Ignatius Press, 2010), 189–191.

10. John F. Thornton and Susan B. Vareene, eds., *The Essential Pope Benedict XVI: His Central Writings and Speeches* (San Francisco: Harper Collins, 2007), 17.

11. Ibid., 25–29.

12. Ibid.

13. Ibid.

14. Ibid.

15. Ibid.

16. Cardinal Joseph Ratzinger/Pope Benedict XVI, *Credo for Today* (San Francisco: Ignatius Press, 2009), 9–12, 17.

17. Ibid., 195–197, 199–200.

18. Pope Benedict XVI, *The Virtues* (Huntington, IN: Our Sunday Visitor Publishing Division, 2010), 23–24.

19. Ibid., 39–40.

20. Ibid., 62, 68.

21. Ibid., 78.

22. Ibid., 79.

23. Ibid., 86, 93, 95, 96.

24. Cardinal Joseph Ratzinger, *Introduction to Christianity* (San Francisco: Ignatius Press, 2004), 11–13.

25. Ibid., 29.

26. Seewald, *Benedict XVI, Light of the World*, xii-xiii.

27. Mansfield, *Pope Benedict XVI: His Life and Mission*, 166.

CONCLUSION

A DOCTRINE FOR TODAY

On April 19, 2005, just three days after his 78th birthday, Cardinal Bishop Joseph Ratzinger was elected pope in a swift election by the conclave of cardinals, taking the name Pope Benedict XVI. On May 7, 2005, in his Homily at the Basilica of Saint John in Lateran, Rome, Pope Benedict XVI said of the papacy, "The pope isn't an absolute sovereign, whose thoughts and desires are law. On the contrary, the ministry of the pope is the guarantor of the obedience toward Christ and his Word. . . . The pope must not proclaim his own idea, but ever link himself and the church to obedience to the Word of God, when faced with all attempts of adaptation or of watering down, as with all opportunism."[1]

Throughout the history of the Church, every new pope has stirred a certain amount of drama within the confines of the Vatican and within the worldwide Church itself. A new pope also affords a sense of wonder to the hierarchy and in the pilgrims who make their way into the church. What new possibilities might occur? What changes will be instituted and why? How will current challenges affect how the new pope reigns? How will he manage the social issues that affect all the religious of the world? How will the pope's age affect how he reigns and wields

Pope Benedict XVI sprinkles holy water during the Pentecost Mass at Saint Peter's Basilica in Rome on May 23, 2010. (AP Photo/Gregorio Borgia)

his mighty power over the Church? What is known is that the occupant of the Chair of Peter, the man who is the leader of the Roman Catholic Church, has a unique view of humanity. However, unlike political and business leaders or world-renowned entertainers, who see the world on their own particular terms, popes see the world in all its decency and sins through Catholic dogma, beliefs, and doctrine that date back over 2,000 years of church history, back to the original pope, Saint Peter. Throughout history, popes have made their papacy their own, a fit to their own wills and to the power of their faith. In addition, popes have been significantly influenced by world events, such as war, scandals, and changing views on popular beliefs. It could be said that the man elected to wear the Fisherman's Ring, the ring given to each pope upon his election, carries the sins of the world on his shoulders and he always stands in the heightened glare of world attention. He is known as the Vicar of Christ, the Chief Priest of Roman Catholicism, and the voice of God to millions of Catholic pilgrims throughout the world.

The papacy of Pope Benedict XVI, the 265th Supreme Pontiff of the Roman Catholic Church, was expected by some to be an interim papacy.

After all, he was the oldest man elected to the papacy in more than two centuries. He also had been in difficult health at several points during the last few years. Before long, however, it was clear his papacy was going to be significant, in part because he is exceptionally driven by his deep convictions in Church doctrine and dogma, altogether based on his years as a theologian and academic. Benedict XVI's papacy is also driven by his years as the regulator of Catholic theology as prefect of the CDF, and by the continuing quantity of issues facing the Church. The expectation of a significant papacy was held even with the inevitable comparison to his predecessor, the immensely popular John Paul II, a man Benedict XVI worked closely with for more than a quarter of a century.

From the very beginning of his papacy, Benedict XVI had a deep theological and cultural preparation. He brought to the Church a clear-eyed view of religion and courage of his convictions from a faith that began with the unique circumstances of his birth. He is a man who fluently speaks seven languages and understands Portuguese. He can read ancient Greek and biblical Hebrew. He enjoys wearing red leather shoes, made by his personal cobbler. He has a pilot's license and likes to fly the Papal helicopter. He has never obtained his driver's license. He loves animals and has a special affinity for cats, having had two of his own. He is known to pause and think before he answers a question, and provides his own clear understanding to his answers to world problems and the problems that the Catholic Church faces. He has written more than 100 theological works.

Pope Benedict XVI is arguably one of the most powerful men in the world, and with his election in April 2005, he has celebrated his seventh year as pope in 2012. As pope, Benedict XVI continually puts his own indelible mark on the Church and on history. He has personally lived through great suffering during World War II, was conscripted into the German Army and was a P.O.W. at the end of the war; he has witnessed the end of communism, and holds a world view that is part optimism and part a warning of what may occur if there is no love, faith, or joy in the Lord. For Benedict XVI, as Christians, there is always a battle of two kinds of love—the false love and a love that is the key to Christianity.

Benedict XVI possesses an eagerness to win over the world to what he says is the beauty of truth, the joy of faith. He is more a scholar than a shepherd to his immense flock and seems to realize he is not as charismatic as his predecessor; however, he possesses a nimble brilliant mind and a humble manner that he uses to compensate for his innate shyness and even to push him a bit further to compensate for his lack of popular appeal. That is not to say he is not considered popular, for he is, drawing vast crowds wherever and whenever he travels or when he presides over mass at the Vatican or speaks to the pilgrims that always gather in Saint Peter's Square at the Vatican. Benedict XVI knows about the world, with its 24-hour news cycles and its technology-driven populace. He knows he leads the Church at a time when the modern world is religiously suspicious.

Since his election in 2005, he has been defining his image and his life, guiding the Church based on the theology that has always dictated his life. And instead of living towards a retirement in his beloved Bavaria, as he had hoped before the death of John Paul and before his election as pope, he will be on the throne of Saint Peter until another pope is elected to define his own world and his papacy. With a population of approximately 1.2 billion, there are more believers in the Catholic Church today than ever before. The Catholic Church encompasses more races than ever before, is a presence on more continents, and is a part of more cultures than at any point in time in our history. However, Pope Benedict XVI believes that these numbers do not give him more power.

Benedict XVI believes, "The pope is on the one hand, a completely powerless man; on the other hand, he bears a great responsibility. He is to a certain extent the leader, the representative, and the one responsible for making sure that the faith that keeps people together is believed, that is remains alive, and that its identity is inviolate."[2]

Pope Benedict XVI has always believed that the "Holy Mother Church is both refuge and answer," and he will be willing, as he always has, "for the Church to be pruned by either apostasy or the sharp sword of orthodoxy, if she will rise again to greatness." For Benedict XVI has often said, "The essential things in history begin always with the small, more convinced communities. So the Church begins with the twelve Apostles. . . . Smaller number, I think, but from these smaller numbers we will have a radiation of joy in the world."[3]

Pope Benedict XVI has often been described as an intellectual; however, he is more than that. Knowledge through study and reading are not, for him, an end to itself, and the scope of study is not limited to in-depth studies or learned discourses. According to Benedict XVI, "Christian faith is not a kind of knowledge but rather it is trust and joy, someone who is glad from the bottom of his heart, who has suffered and has not lost the capacity for joy, cannot be far from the God of the gospel, whose first word at the threshold of the New Covenant is: Rejoice. . . . Christian faith is not an ideology, not a world view or philosophy. It is in the first place a gift, a present, and therefore something that was given to us, something that we have received and have to preserve. For we ourselves did not make the faith and its contents, and we cannot arbitrarily change it any way we like, but rather as human beings we must make room in our lives and thoughts for the truth of the faith."[4]

NOTES

1. Stephen Mansfield, *Pope Benedict XVI: His Life and Mission* (New York: Jeremy P. Tarcher/Penguin, 2005), 165.

2. Peter Seewald, *Benedict XVI, Light of the World* (San Francisco: Ignatius Press, 2010), 6–7.

3. Mansfield, *Pope Benedict XVI: His Life and Mission*, 162.

4. Cardinal Joseph Ratzinger, *Credo for Today: What Christians Believe* (San Francisco: Ignatius Press, 2009), 201–203.

ADDENDUM

"... I have had to recognize my incapacity to adequately
fulfill the ministry entrusted to me."

The first pope to use Twitter as a means of communicating with the
world's Catholics, Pope Benedict XVI sent a Twitter message to his followers, dated February 11, 2013, saying—"All have sinned and fall short
of the glory of God," from Romans 3:23 (PopeBenedictXVI@Pope-
BenedictXVI).[1] That same day, at the end of a routine assembly of cardinals to discuss the canonizations of three potential saints, Pope Benedict
XVI, speaking softly in Latin, announced his decision to resign as pope
and as the leader of the world's 1.2 billion Catholics. As of that moment,
he became the first modern pope to abdicate and the first pope since the
Middle Ages to step down from the chair of Saint Peter. Giving some a
pause to consider a possible message, and to others, who considered it an
interesting coincidence, later in the evening, during a thunderstorm in
Rome, a bolt of lightning struck the dome of Saint Peter's Basilica.

In his statement to the cardinals, Pope Benedict XVI said:

> After having repeatedly examined my conscience before God, I
> have come to the certainty that my strengths due to an advanced

age are no longer suited to an adequate exercise of the Petrine ministry. I am well aware that this ministry, due to its essential spiritual nature, must be carried out not only by words and deeds but no less with prayer and suffering. However, in today's world, subject to so many rapid changes and shaken by questions of deep relevance for the life of faith, in order to govern the barque of St. Peter and proclaim the Gospel, both strength of mind and body are necessary, strengths which in the last few months, has deteriorated in me to the extent that I have had to recognize my incapacity to adequately fulfill the ministry entrusted to me.[2]

Pope Benedict ended his statement: "With regard to myself, I wish to also devotedly serve the Holy Church of God in the future through a life dedicated to prayer."[3] He said the resignation would take effect on February 28, 2013, at 8:00 p.m., Rome time. Pope Benedict XVI's statement, delivered at the end of what was thought to be a routine meeting, stunned the assembled cardinals. Just after the meeting, as news traveled throughout the Vatican, many of the pope's closest aides were incredulous. Due to the immediacy of news reports through various means of communication and media outlets, the news traveled quickly and it shocked the world. Within minutes, #Pontifexit was trending on Twitter.

It was soon evident that even the pope's own cardinals and a Vatican spokesman, Rev. Federico Lombardi, were taken by surprise, although Lombardi noted that while it was a surprise, he was not shocked. As he put it at a press conference, Pope Benedict XVI had broached the topic in a book-length interview with a German journalist. Lombardi quoted the pope's words—"When a Pope understands clearly that he is no longer physically, mentally and spiritually capable of carrying out the mission that has been entrusted to him, he has the right, and in some circumstances even the duty, to resign."[4] By the next day, other signs of an impending resignation came to light, including the ongoing renovation of a building on the Vatican grounds. It soon became known that this was where Pope Benedict XVI would soon live. Vatican spokesman Greg Burke said the decision to step down did not come as a complete surprise to Vatican officials, "who have known at least several weeks."[5] According to Giovanni Maria Via, the editor of the Vatican newspaper, *L'Osservatore Romano*, the pope's decision "was taken many months ago," after a trip to Mexico and Cuba in March 2012, "and kept with a reserve that no one could violate."[6] In recent months, the pope had been showing signs of age, often seeming tired. He was also being taken to the altar of Saint Peter's on a wheeled platform instead of walking the aisle as he always had. Despite this, few expected him to suddenly resign.

Reactions to the news were swift. From world leaders to worshipers entering their local church to attend daily mass, there was disbelief, relief, sorrow, and acceptance, with thoughts ranging from the pope as a good caretaker, to a pope difficult to love, to a pope who is humble and brave to make such a decision. The news prompted reactions from around the world including a statement from President Barack Obama, where he said, "Michelle and I warmly remember our meeting with the Holy Father in 2009, and I have appreciated our work together over these last four years." The leader of the archdiocese of Westminster, which includes parts of London, England, Vincent Nichols, said the pope's announcement "has shocked and surprised everyone . . . Yet, on reflection, I am sure that many will recognize it to be a decision of great courage and characteristic clarity of mind and action." The archbishop of Canterbury, Justin Welby, stated he learned of the news "with a heavy heart but complete understanding." The archbishop of Washington, Cardinal Donald Wuerl said that he had been working on his homily early in the morning when he received a call and learned of the pope's decision; he added that it had come as an "enormous surprise" and that "Transitions in the church are not new. With each passing pontificate, the church turns to filling the See of Peter. And this has gone on for 2,000 years, so this will not be a new experience."[7]

Other reactions included that of the Chancellor of Germany, Angela Merkel, who recalled the pride that Germany felt to see one of their own elected by his fellow cardinals, but also expressed understanding that he could not continue. Merkel said, "In our age of ever longer lives, many people will also be able to understand how the Pope must deal with the burdens of aging." The archbishop emeritus of Gdansk in northern Poland said, "It came as a bolt out of the blue." The archbishop of Dublin, Diarmuid Martin, said that the pope would be mainly remembered for his writings on theology and that the pope "had a very clear understanding of some of the moral problems confronting the church and he had addressed them 'head on.' I have a great personal affection for the pope, I have known him for many, many years, and I'm not surprised that he would take a decision of this kind if he felt that the burden he was under was too much." A former student of the pope, the Rev. Vincent Twomey, now a theologian in Ireland, said the pontiff did not look well last summer. "We all felt he looked gray and tired, and shriveled, to a certain extent. Then he came the following day and said Mass for us and then joined us for breakfast." Msgr. Georg Ratzinger said his brother was having increasing difficulty walking, and that his doctor had advised against any more transatlantic journeys. He said, "My brother wants more peace in old age."[8]

Pope Benedict XVI is known as a brilliant academic and a strict conservative. He has also been labeled "the Pope of Surprises" due his unpredictability. Despite this label, and in consideration of his apparent declining health at 85 years of age, few imagined he would ever resign. The news stunned so many and was seemingly so unheard of in the modern age of popes, where newly elected popes are elected only after a pope dies, especially in light of Pope Benedict XVI's mentor and predecessor, Pope John Paul, who suffered from dire health conditions and continued to carry on; the news almost immediately prompted speculation about other reasons for his unexpected decision. However, those close to the pope quickly argued that the decision was very much in keeping with his character. Thought to be a reluctant pope in the first place, having once remarked that on learning of his election, he felt like a guillotine had come down on his neck, Benedict XVI courageously embraced it. But it was no secret that when he served as a cardinal years ago, he had dreams of retiring and spending time in his native Bavaria writing books, playing the piano, and praying and studying. For Pope Benedict XVI, a man known for his humility and a pope keenly aware of his strengths and his frailties, he had earlier alluded to the fact that he would consider resigning if he felt it was the right time. The pope himself raised the possibility of resigning if he were too old or too sick to continue when he was interviewed by Peter Seewald in 2010 for the book, *Light of the World.*

Popes are allowed to resign. Church law specifies only that the resignation be "freely made and properly manifested." However, in papacy history, only a few have done so and there is one good reason why—for when two popes exist at the same time, when one has stepped down and another is elected by the conclave of cardinals, it may lead to divisions and instability in the church.[9] Pope Benedict XVI's resignation immediately set in motion a complex transition period with questions never before addressed that needed to be answered.

The Vatican announced that the conclave to choose a new leader of the Church was expected to begin in mid-March—15 to 20 days after Pope Benedict XVI stepped down; a new pope could possibly be elected before Easter, March 31, 2013. However, National Public Radio's Sylvia Poggioli reported that it was unclear how the Church would function with two living popes. John Allen, Vatican analyst for the *National Catholic Reporter*, stated, "The fear that having simultaneous Popes would risk dividing the church. That is, you would have one camp loyal to the old, one camp loyal to the new one and some saw that as a church enforced schism." Having a retired pope while another is serving as pope is new to the Vatican and a situation the Church has not dealt with in modern times. Allen continued: "And so, exactly what his role will be (Pope Benedict), when we will see him in public, whether he will travel, whether he will continue to write books and indulge his taste for theology—these are all questions that are going to have to be sorted out in the days and weeks to come." According to Vatican spokesman Rev. Federico Lombardi, "(Pope) Benedict will not take part in the conclave and will have no role in choosing his successor." Robert Mickens, Vatican correspondent of the Catholic weekly, *The Tablet*, stated, "Benedict could have a great influence on the cardinals who have sworn allegiance and obedience to him . . . And it's going to be difficult for cardinals to choose somebody who would have a vision of the church that would vary in any way from the plan or the trajectory that Benedict XVI has put the Roman Catholic Church on these last eight years.[10] On February 13, 2013, Lombardi stated, "The pope will surely say absolutely nothing about the process of the election. He will not interfere in any way." As for the pope's new title, Greg Burke, the Vatican's senior communications adviser, said he would most likely be referred to as "Bishop of Rome, emeritus," as opposed to "Pope Emeritus."[11]

Once the news of the resignation began to settle, plans began for the election of a new pope by the conclave of the cardinals. The process known as "interregnum" was set to begin on February 28, 2013, at 8:00 p.m., the precise time set by Pope Benedict XVI for when the See of Saint Peter would be vacant. This period typically begins upon the death of a pope and after a period of mourning. For the duration of the election process, Pope Benedict XVI will leave the Vatican and travel to the papal summer home in Castel Gandolfo, where he will spend time resting and praying. Once the process ends and a new pope is elected, Pope Benedict XVI will move back to a four-story building attached to a monastery on the northern edge of the Vatican gardens, where cloistered nuns once lived. To assist in the transition process and prepare for the conclave, the members of the College of Cardinals were called to Rome. Of those members, only those under the age of 80, or a total of 117, are eligible to vote in the conclave.[12] All of the voting cardinals have been chosen either by Pope Benedict XVI or his predecessor, Pope John Paul II.

As the news spread throughout the world, so did the speculation about the possible papal candidates. Several names seemed to be in consideration, including the Italian cardinal Angelo Scola, archbishop of Milan; Cardinal Marc Ouellet, the Canadian who runs the Vatican department for bishops; Argentinean cardinal Leonardo Sandri, who was chief of staff of John Paul II; and the Brazilian cardinal, Odilo Pedro Scherer, who has European roots and comes from the largest Catholic country in the world.[13]

"IN FULL LIBERTY FOR THE GOOD OF THE CHURCH"

On Wednesday, February 13, 2013, in his first public appearance since his resignation announcement, Pope Benedict XVI said he made his decision "in full liberty for the good of the church," because he no longer had the strength needed to carry out the duties of the papacy. Wearing simple white robes and a skullcap, the pope spoke in Italian to a general audience at the Vatican. As he entered the Paul VI audience hall, he was greeted with a standing ovation by a crowd of nearly 8,000 people. A banner proclaimed *"Grazie Santita"* or "Thank you, Your Holiness."

The Pope smiled and thanked the Italian children's choice, who sang for him in German, telling them, "The gift of singing songs is particularly dear to me." The pope explained that before reaching his decision to resign, he had prayed and examined his conscience. He said he had been "well aware of the seriousness of this act, but also aware of the fact that I am no longer capable of carrying out Peter's Ministry with the strength needed. The certainty that the church belongs to God supports and illuminates me, and Christ will always give his guidance and care. I thank you all for your love and prayer with which you've accompanied me. Please keep praying for the pope and the church. I felt it almost physically, throughout these days that were not easy for me. Keep praying for me, for the church and for the future pope. The Lord will guide us."[14]

Later in the day, Pope Benedict XVI celebrated Ash Wednesday at a filled-to-capacity Saint Peter's Basilica—a change of venue from the smaller church where the usual Ash Wednesday service is held, due to the anticipated larger crowd. Pope Benedict XVI filed into Saint Peter's behind a procession of cardinals and then stood on his wheeled platform, which allowed him to be among the congregants. The mood inside the Basilica was somber; yet, when the pope exited, a minute-long standing ovation erupted. Cardinal Tarcisio Bertone, the pope's longtime deputy, told the pope at the end of the service, "We wouldn't be sincere, Your Holiness, if we didn't tell you that there's a veil of sadness on our hearts this evening. Thank you for having given us the luminous example of the simple and humble worker in the vineyard of the Lord." The crowd yelled, "*Viva il papa!*"[15]

NOTES

1. https://twitter.com/PopeBenedictXVI.

2. Daniela Petroff, "Pope Benedict XVI to Resign on Feb. 28 Due to Health Concerns," *Associated Press*, February 11, 2013.

3. "Pope Benedict XVI announces his resignation at end of month," *Vatican Radio*, http://en.radiovaticana.va. February 11, 2013.

4. Sylvia Poggioli, "Simultaneous Popes Could Disrupt Catholic Church," http:// www.npr.org, February 11, 2013.

5. Erin McClam, *NBC News*, http://worldnews.nbcnews.com, February 12, 2013.

6. Rachel Donadio and Nicholas Kulish, "A Statement Rocks Rome, Then Sends Shockwaves Around the World," *New York Times*, February 12, 2013.

7. Ibid.

8. Nicholas Kulish, "Catholics react with shock, sympathy and muted criticism," *New York Times*, February 12, 2013.

9. Daniela Petroff, "Pope Benedict XVI to Resign on Feb. 28 Due to Health Concerns."

10. Sylvia Poggioli, "Simultaneous Popes Could Disrupt Catholic Church."

11. "Pacemaker put in pope decade ago, Vatican says," *The Denver Post*, February 13, 2013, 18A.

12. Carol Glatz and John Thavis, "Pope Benedict's resignation will set in motion period of transition," *National Catholic Reporter*, http://ncronline.org, February 12, 2013.

13. Sylvia Poggioli, "Simultaneous Popes Could Disrupt Catholic Church."

14. Elisabetta Povoledo and Alan Cowell, "Pope Says Exit Is For 'Good of the Church,'" *New York Times*, February 13, 2013.

15. Nicole Winfield, "Pope Benedict XVI Resignation: Pontiff Says He's Resigning for the 'Good of the Church,'" Huffington Post Online, http://www.huffingtonpost.com, February 13, 2013.

BIBLIOGRAPHY

Akin, Jimmy. "Holy See Mandates Reform of U.S. Women Religious' Conference." *National Catholic Register*, April 19, 2012, http://www.ncregister.com.

Allen, John L., Jr. *Cardinal Ratzinger*. New York: The Continuum International Publishing Group, Inc., 2000.

Allen, John L., Jr. "Not a Transitional Pope: Benedict May Surprise." *National Catholic Reporter*, April 29, 2005, 5–8.

Allen, John L., Jr. *The Rise of Benedict XVI*. New York: Doubleday, 2005.

Benedict, Pope. *Benedict XVI, Light of the World*. San Francisco: Ignatius Press, 2010.

Bethune, Brian. "Is the Pope Catholic?" *Macleans*, April 18, 2011, www2.macleans.ca/2011/04/18/rebel-with-a-cross.

"Cardinal Joseph Ratzinger Elected Pope Benedict XVI." *America* 192, no. 15, May 2, 2005, 4–6.

Collins, Michael. *Pope Benedict XVI: The First Five Years*. Dublin, Ireland: The Columba Press, 2010.

"Continued Pain Over Kristallnacht." *America*, November 24, 2008, 6+.

Desmond, Joan Frawley. "Bishops Defend Legal Strategy as HHS Mandate Emerges as Election-Year Issue." *National Catholic Register,* May 30, 2012, http://www.ncregister.com.

Desmond, Joan Frawley. "Installed at Baltimore's Cathedral, Archbishop Lori Draws Line in Sand for Courageous Faith." *National Catholic Register,* May 17, 2012, http://www.ncregister.com.

Donadio, Rachel. "Vatican Inquiry Finds Progress in Irish Abuse Scandal." *New York Times,* March 20, 2012, www.nytimes.com.

Duffy, Eamon. *Saints & Sinners: A History of the Popes.* New Haven, CT: Yale University Press, 1997.

Fox, Matthew. *The Pope's War.* New York: Sterling Ethos, 2011.

Gibbs, Nancy, and Jordan Bonfante, et al. "The New Shepherd." *Time,* May 2, 2005, 28.

Gibson, Dave. "10 Years After Catholic Sex Abuse Reforms, What's Changed?" *Huffington Post Online,* June 7, 2012, http://www.huffingtonpost.com.

Grenholm, Cristina. "A New Pope and Voices That Deviate from the Norm." *Dialog: A Journal of Theology* (Fall 2005): 304–306.

Hesemann, Michael. "Brothers in Faith: How the Ratzinger Boys Became World Catholic Leaders." *The Huffington Post Online,* March 1, 2012, http://www.huffingtonpost.com.

Hooda, Samreen. "Birth Control Morally Acceptable to Catholics, Most Americans." *The Huffington Post Online,* June 7, 2012, http://www.huffingtonpost.com.

"How Will Benedict Rule?" *U.S. Catholic* 70, June 2005, 30–34.

Kelly, J.N.D., and M.J. Walsh. *Oxford Dictionary of Popes.* Oxford: Oxford University Press, 1986.

Mansfield, Stephen. *Pope Benedict XVI: His Life and Mission.* New York: Jeremy P. Tarcher/Pengiun, 2005.

McBrien, Richard P. *Lives of the Popes.* San Francisco: HarperSanFrancisco, 1997.

McDowell, Bart. *Inside the Vatican.* Washington, DC: National Geographic Society, 1991.

Newman, Scott. "Nuns and the Vatican: A Clash Decades in Making." *NPR,* May 3, 2012, http://www.npr.org.

Noonan, Peggy. *John Paul the Great.* New York: Viking, 2005.

Original Catholic Encyclopedia. http://www.oce.catholic.com.

Pogatchnik, Shawn. "Catholics Find Skeptics." *The Denver Post*, June 11, 2012, 12A.

Pope Benedict XVI. Encyclical Letter, *Deus Caritas Est*. December 25, 2005, http://www.vatican.va.

Pope Benedict XVI. *The Virtues*. Huntington, IN: One Sunday Visitor Publishing Division, Our Sunday Visitor, Inc., 2010.

"Pope Recalls Holocaust as Darkest Period." *America*, September 12, 2005, 6.

"Pope Reflects on the Power of Prayer." *National Catholic Register*, May 9, 2012, http://www.ncregister.com.

"Pope 'Working Harder Than Anyone' at Synod Sessions." *National Catholic Register*, October 10, 2012, http://www.ncregister.com.

Pullella, Philip. "Pope Denounces U.S. Efforts to Legalize Gay Marriage." *Huffington Post Online*, March 9, 2012, http://www.huffingtonpost.com.

Ratzinger, Georg. *My Brother, the Pope*. San Francisco: Ignatius Press, 2011.

Ratzinger, Cardinal Joseph/Pope Benedict XVI. *Credo for Today: What Christians Believe*. San Francisco: Ignatius Press, 2009.

Ratzinger, Cardinal Joseph. *Introduction to Christianity*. San Francisco: Ignatius Press, 2004.

Ratzinger, Cardinal Joseph. *Salt of the Earth: Christianity and the Catholic Church at the End of the Millennium*. San Francisco: Ignatius Press, 2005.

Ratzinger, Joseph. *Milestones*. San Francisco: Ignatius Press, 1998.

"Remembering Blessed John Paul II One Year On." *National Catholic Register*, April 30, 2012, http://www.ncregister.com.

Ryback, Timothy W. "Forgiveness." *The New Yorker*, February 6, 2006, 66.

Seewald, Peter. *Benedict XVI, Light of the World: A Conversation with Peter Seewald*. San Francisco: Ignatius Press, 2010.

Simon, Stephanie. "Vatican Crackdown on Nuns Over Social Justice Issues, Women Ordination." *Reuters*, April 20, 2012, http://www.huffingtonpostonline.

Sullivan, Andrew. "The Vatican's New Stereotype." *Time*, December 12, 2005, 92.

Thornton, John F., and Susan B. Vareene, eds. *The Essential Pope Benedict XVI: His Central Writings and Speeches*. San Francisco: Harper Collins, 2007.

"Timeline of Pope Benedict XVI's Pontificate." *National Catholic Register*, April 20, 2010, http://www.ncregister.com.

Tobin, Greg. *Holy Father*. New York: Sterling Publishing, Co., Inc., 2005.

"U.S. Bishops, Apostolates Ring in the Year of Faith." *National Catholic Register*, October 10, 2012, http://www.ncregister.com.

"Vatican Blames Lack of Priests on Secularism, Abuse, Parents." *Huffington Post*, June 25, 2012, http://www.huffingtonpost.com.

"Vatican: Pope Presses U.S. Bishops on Message on Sex." *Associated Press*, March 10, 2012, http://www.nytimes.com.

Vatican: The Holy See. http://www.vaticanstate.va.

Weigel, George. *God's Choice: Pope Benedict XVI and the Future of the Catholic Church*. New York: Harper Collins, 2005.

Wilkinson, Philip. *Illustrated Dictionary of Religions*. London: Dorling Kindersley Limited, 1999.

Winfield, Nichole, and Daniela Petroff. "Pope Celebrates a Very Bavarian 85th Birthday." Associated Press, April 16, 2012, http://www.huffingtonpost.com.

Wooden, Cindy. "Statistically Speaking: Vatican Numbers Hint at Fading Faith Practice," *National Catholic Reporter*, August 17, 2012, http://ncronline.org.

INDEX

Academic career, 55–61: Chair
    for dogmatic and fundamental
    theology, 56; father's illness,
    60; *Habilitation*, work on,
    56–58; lectures as a professor
    of fundamental theology, 59;
    professor at the University of
    Bonn, 59–61; study of music,
    58–59
Affordable Care Act, 2010,
    102–3
Anti-Semitic outrages, 1933, 36
Archbishop of Munich and
    Freising, 75–76; *Cooperatores
    Veritatis* or "Co-worker of the
    Truth," 76
Ascendance of Pope Benedict
    XVI, 91–110: challenges and
    issues, 93; Church doctrine,

theology, and faith, 93–94;
    John Paul II's legacy, 92; lead-
    ing Church according to its
    history, 93; and modern tech-
    nology, 91; social issues and
    Catholic Church Doctrine,
    94–110; spiritual depth, 92

Baptism and childhood, 26, 54
Bavarian Catholicism, 27
Bible and theology, study of, 48
Biblical scholarship, 83
Birth control and Church,
    101–4: "accommodation,"
    Obama's administration, 103;
    Affordable Care Act, 2010,
    102–3; co-pay-free abortion
    drugs, 103; First Amendment–
    religious freedom issue, 102–3;

Light of the World, 103–4;
Lori's installation, 102–3;
Succisa virescit, or "pruned, it
grows again," 101–2
Boff case, 85
The Boston Globe, 2002, 94

Catechism of the Catholic Church,
89, 127
Catholic Education, 84, 106
Catholic student movement, 17
Celibacy, practice of, 104
Charter for the Protection of
Children and Young People
("Dallas Charter"), 97–98
Christian Unity, 16, 84, 100
Church and Evangelism,
99–101: Benedict XVI's pa-
pacy, 99; Catholic identity
and purpose, 100; pastoral
activities, 99–100; *Porta
Fidei* (Door of Faith), 100;
"renewed evangelical dyna-
mism," 100–101; *The Virtues*,
101; Year of Faith, 100
Church: Charisma and Power
(Boff), 85
*The Church With a Human Face:
A New and Expanded Theology
of Ministry* (Schillebeeckx),
87
Code of Canon Law, 6, 84
Communion, 8, 42, 74, 89, 105
Congregation for the Doctrine of
the Faith (CDF), 23, 40, 77,
79, 81–89, 93, 107, 109–10,
113–15, 125, 131

Co-pay-free abortion drugs, 103
Credo for Today, 121: The
Church's Credo (essay),
121–23; What It Means to
Be a Christian, Over Every-
thing: Love (essay), 121
Curran case, 85–87

Dachau memorial, 38
The Denver Post, 2012, 97
Doctrinal integrity (*Pastor
Bonus*, 1988 apostolic consti-
tution), 84
Dogmatic Constitution of the
Church, 68

Early years: anti-Semitic outrages, 1933, 36; arrival of
the archbishop, 29; Bavarian
Catholicism, 27; childhood
and baptism, 26; conscript in
German Army, 33; friendship
of Cardinal Ratzinger, 34;
"humanistic" *gymnasium*, 31;
issues of Church, Popes and
Jews, 36–43; love of music,
27–28; military career, 33–34;
minor seminary, 31; Nazi
movement, 28–30; parents,
25–26; radio operator in the
signal corps, 32; Treaty of
Versailles, 27; war years, 35
Election, popes, 4–6: absolute
monarch of Catholic Church,
6; Catholic cardinals, 5; Code
of Canon Law for the removal
of pope, 6; competition and

compromise, 5; direct successor of Saint Peter, 4; majority of two-thirds vote (Pope John Paul II changed), 6; personal, human, and spiritual considerations, 5; political beliefs and personal biases, 6; promises that benefit cardinal groups, 5

Encyclical letters, 117–18: *Caritas in Veritate*, 2009 (third letter), 118; *Deus Caritas Est* or "God is Love," 2005 (first letter), 117; *Spe Salvi*, 2007 (second letter), 118

Eucharistic congress, 97

"The Family" report, discussion on birth control, 77

Fascism in Italy, 11–13

Feminist movement, 107

Fertility and procreation, 101

First Amendment–religious freedom issue, 102–3

First sermon, 52

Five Vatican congregations, 83–84

Gay marriage: to legalize in the United States, 105; powerful gay marriage lobby in America, 105–6; sexual orientation, 104

Habilitation, work on, 56–58

Herzogliches Gregorianum, theological institute, 47

Hitler's Pope, 37

Hitler Youth program, 38, 42

Holy See, 1–3, 9, 84, 89, 109

Homilies and books, 120–27: *Credo for Today*, 121; first homily, 2005, 120–21; "Follow Me" (homily), 120; homily at funeral mass for John Paul II, 2005, 120; inaugural homily at Saint Peter's Square in Rome, 127; *Introduction to Christianity*, 1968, 125; *Light of the World*, 127; other works, 126–27; *The Virtues*, 123–24

The Huffington Post Online, 98

"Humanistic" *gymnasium*, 31

Inside the Vatican (Bart McDowell), 2

International Papal Theological Commission, 73

Introduction to Christianity, 1968, 72–73, 125–26

The Irish Times, 97

Jews issues, 36–43: atrocities against Jews by Nazis, 38; connection to the Nazi regime, 37; Dachau memorial, 38; diplomatic relations with Israel, 37; Hitler's Pope, 37; Hitler Youth program, 42; Marshall Plan, 40; Prefect of CDF, 40; pro-Nazi Vichy regime, 37; relationship between Catholics and Jews, 37–38; Roman synagogue,

visit to, 37; visit to France to
deliver papal blessings, 39;
visit to the small cemetery,
39–40
Journal *Dialogue: A Journal of
Theology*, 108

Kristallnacht pogrom, 1938, 40

Lateran Treaty, 3–4, 11
Leadership Conference of
Women Religious (LCWR),
109–10
*Letter to the Bishops of the Catholic
Church on the Pastoral Care of
Homosexual Persons*, 87
Light of the World, 103–4, 127

Major seminary at Freising:
called to ministries, 54;
Church liturgy and worship,
46; doctoral coursework, 55;
lectures to seminary students,
55; Michael Höck, "the
Father," 46–47; study with
battle-hardened men, 46
Marriage and Church, 101:
fertility and procreation, 101;
"Marriage as Instrument of
Salvation," 101
Marshall Plan, 40
Mieth, Dietmar (German moral
theologian), 108–9
Milestones, Memoirs 1927–1977,
33
Military career, 33–34
Minor seminary, 31

Missal of Paul VI, 74
Motto "Christ's peace in Christ's
kingdom," 11
Music, love of, 27–28
My brother, the Pope, 36, 41–42

Nazism: in Germany, 11; glow
of alps and gloom of, 26–32;
Nazi movement, 28–30; racist
doctrines (Hitler's), 12

Oriental Churches, 83

"Panzer Cardinal," 82, 90
Parish of the Precious Blood,
assistant pastor, 52–54: Father
Blumschein, model of his
pastoral work, 54; schedule, 53
Pastoral Guidelines for Fostering
Vocations to Priestly Ministry
(document), 106
Pastoral letters, 119: "Seri-
ous Sins against Defenseless
Children," 2010, 119
Pastoral ministry: assistant
pastor at the Parish of the
Precious Blood, 52–54; Father
Ratzinger as professor, 55–61;
new assignment in Freising,
54–55
Perspectives of Pope Benedict
XVI, 113–27: Bishop of
Rome, 120; encyclical letters, 117–18; homilies and
books, 120–27; pastoral letters, 119; position of Prefect
of the CDF, 113; *Salt of the*

Earth, 115–17; service to the Church, 114–15; theological writing, 113–14; tight scheduled responsibilities, 117

Pius X (1835–1914), 7–8: chancellor of his home diocese of Treviso, 7; changes during Pius X' reign, 8; named patriarch of Venice and a cardinal, 7; simplification of the Code of Cannon Law, 8; 255th pope, 7

Pius XII (1876–1958): be pro-Italian and pro-German, 13; clear denunciation of the Jewish genocide, 13; condemn Nazi policies, 13; negotiated peace agreement, 13; pastoral and religious activities, 14; Vatican's involvement with the war, 14

Pope Benedict XV (1854–1922), 8–10: diplomatic experience, 9; encouraged Catholics to join the trade union movements, 10; service to poor and wounded, 9–10; studies, 9; 256th pope, 8

Pope John Paul I (1912–1978): dual name, 19; implementation of Second Vatican Council, 20; served as pope, 1978, 19–20

Pope John Paul II (1920–2005): Cardinal Ratzinger as next pope, 24; contributions to religious freedom, 21;

diplomatic relations with Israel, 22; global mission of his papacy, 22; mercy to one another in encyclical, 21; professor, 20; promote the teachings of the Second Vatican Council, 21; religious liberty, 21

Pope John XXIII (1881–1963): Christian unity, 16; encyclicals, 16; genial diplomat, 15; Presidential Medal of Freedom, 17; reasons for the name, 15–16; Second Vatican Council, 16; served as pope during 1958–1963, 15–17

Pope Paul VI (1897–1978): Cardinal Montini, 17–18; Catholic student movement, 17; committed to establishing unity, 18; encyclical condemning contraception, 17; Priestly celibacy, 19; reform of the Mass, 18; Synod of Bishops, 18

Pope Pius XI (1857–1939): authoritarian, papal ministry, 12; condemnation of communism, 11; condemned Nazism, 12; fascism in Italy, 11; German and French linguistic proficiency, 10; Hitler's racist doctrines, 12; motto "Christ's peace in Christ's kingdom," 11; Nazisn in Germany, 11; pastoral communication, 11; reconciliation between

the Vatican and the Italian
state, 10
Porta Fidei (Door of Faith), 100
Prefect of CDF, 77–78, 81–90:
Apostolic Visitation in the
Archdiocese of Seattle, 87;
biblical scholarship, 83; Boff
case, 85; CDF ("God's Ge-
stapo"), 82; Code of Canon
Law, 84; communion, 89;
Curran case, 85–86; dean of
the College of Cardinals, 84;
Doctrinal integrity (*Pastor
Bonus*, 1988 apostolic constitution), 84; elected as pope,
2005, 90; excommunication
of Archbishop Thuc, 84–85;
Extraordinary Synod of Bish-
ops, 89; five Vatican congre-
gations, 83–84; history of the
Congregation (Holy Office),
82; issue of sexuality, 87–88;
John Paul II's confidence in
Joseph, 83; "Panzer Cardinal,"
90; Second Vatican Council,
89; service in the German
Army during World War II,
82; titular Bishop of Ostia,
2002, 84; Vatican "foreign
ministry," 84; writings of
Dominican Father Edward
Schillebeeckx, 85–87
Presidential Medal of Freedom,
17
"Priestly celibacy," 19
Pro-Nazi Vichy regime, 37
Protest rally in Munich, 77

"Radical feminism," 109
*The Ratzinger Report: An Exclu-
sive Interview on the State of the
Church*, 68–69, 89
"Renewed evangelical dynamism," 100–101
Rome, path to: Archbishop Of
Munich And Freising, 75–76;
"Dogmatic Constitution of
the Church," 68; "The Family" report, discussion on
birth control, 77; influences,
67–69; member on the editorial committee, 68; Prefect of
the CDF, 77–78; protest rally
in Munich, 77; role as the advisor to Frings, 67–68; role of
the Holy Office, the theory of
bishop collegiality, 68; Second
Vatican Council, 1962–1965,
63–67; University Of Mün-
ster, 69–71; University Of Regensburg, 72–75; University
Of Tübingen, 71–72

Salt of the Earth, 115
Schillebeeckx, writings of,
85–87
Second Vatican Council,
16, 63–67, 89, 109–10:
advancements within the
Church hierarchy, 67; archdiocese of Cologne, 64;
Cardinal Frings, 64; Catholic
doctrines, 66; implementation of, 20; memoir, 64–65;
memoir *Milestones*, 65; Pope

John XXIII, beatified, 64;
pray with Protestants and
attend weddings and fu-
nerals, 65–66; revolution
within Catholicism, 66; 21st
Ecumenical Council of the
Catholic Church, 65
Sexual abuses within the Catholic Church, 94–99: burdens
on Benedict XVI's papacy, 99;
Charter for the Protection of
Children and Young People
("Dallas Charter"), 97–98;
child abuse, 95; eucharistic
congress, 97; Irish charity
("One in Four"), 96; Past
Archbishop Sean Brady of
Armagh, Ireland, 96; preventing crimes, 98–99; scandals
in Ireland, 95–97; scandals
in the United States, 94–95;
sexual abuse by priests, 96
Sistine Chapel (Michelangelo), 4
Social issues and Catholic
Church Doctrine: abuse scandals, Vatican statement about,
106; birth control, 101–4; celibacy, homosexuality, and gay
marriage, 104–6; Evangelism,
99–101; marriage, 101; sexual
abuses, 94–99; sexuality, issue
of, 87–88; women, 106–10
Some Considerations Concerning
the Response to Legislative Proposals on Nondiscrimination of
Homosexual Persons, 88
Swiss Guards of Vatican City, 3

Treaty of Versailles, 27, 40

United Nations Educational,
Scientific, and Cultural Organization (UNESCO), 15
University Of Munich: Bible
and theology, study of, 48;
first sermon, 52; Herzogliches
Gregorianum, theological institute, 47; official installation
ceremony into priesthood,
50–51; traditional day of ordination, 51; views of orthodoxy, 49–50
University Of Münster, 69–71:
involvement in the area of
dogma, 70; time between the
university and Rome, 70–71
University Of Regensburg,
72–75: Communio, inter-
national journal, 74; dogmatic theology book, 74;
International Papal Theo-
logical Commission, 73–74;
lifelong friendship with
Balthasar, 74
University Of Tübingen, 71–72:
Chair in dogma, 72; faculty
members, 72; lectures on "Introduction to Christianity,"
72; position as Chair in fundamental theology, 71

Vatican and Popes of the
modern era: basilica at, 2;
extraterritorial, 4; Holy See,
2; modern popes, 7; popes,

election, 4–6; post office and a radio station, 4; Saint Peter's Basilica—Michelangelo's famous "Pietá," 4; Saint Pius X (1835–1914); Sistine Chapel (Michelangelo), 4; Swiss Guards, 4; visitors, 4

Vatican's Statistical Yearbook of the Church, 1

Viale Vatican, 3

The Virtues, 101, 123–24

Women, 106–10: Catholic nuns, 106–10; CDF doctrinal assessment, 107, 110; feminist movement, 107; LCWR, 109; Mieth, Dietmar (German moral theologian), 108–9; ordination of, 107; radical feminism, 107, 109; Second Vatican Council, 1962–1965, 109–10; themes of "radical feminism," 109; Vatican and American nuns, tensions between, 106–7

World Day of Peace, 117

World Mission Day, 117

World War I, 8–9, 11–12, 15, 27, 48–49

World War II, 11–13, 37–38, 41–42, 63, 82, 131

World Youth Day, 117

Year of Faith, 100

About the Author

Joann F. Price is a professional writer, author, writing coach, and instructor of English with more than 30 years in business, banking and finance, and academic settings. She is the author of *Prince William of Wales: A Biography*; *Barack Obama: A Biography*; *Barack Obama: The Voice of an American Leader*; and *Martha Stewart: A Biography*. Her essay on care giving, entitled "Taking Care," appeared in two volumes of the *Voices* series by The Healing Project, LaChance Publishing. She spends her time with her family, writing, reading, planning trips, and traveling as much as possible.